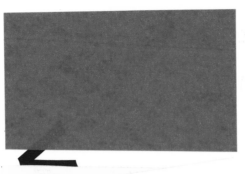

EXPORT

FRAGMENTS OF THE IMAGINATION

Women Artists in Film

Roswitha Mueller and Kaja Silverman, series editors

INDIANA UNIVERSITY PRESS   BLOOMINGTON AND INDIANAPOLIS

VALIE EXPORT

EXPORT

FRAGMENTS OF THE IMAGINATION

ROSWITHA MUELLER

Manufactured in the United States of America

Library of Congress Cataloging-in-Publication Data
Mueller, Roswitha, date
    Valie Export : fragments of the imagination / by Roswitha Mueller.
        p.   cm. — (Women artists in film)
    Filmography and videography: p.
    Includes bibliographical references and index.
    ISBN 0-253-33906-5 (alk. paper) —
    ISBN 0-253-20925-0 (alk. paper: pbk.)
    1. Export, Valie—Criticism and interpretation.
    2. Feminism and the arts—Austria.   I. Title.
    II. Series.
    NX548.Z9E866   1994
    700´.92—dc20

94-6589

1 2 3 4 5 00 99 98 97 96 95 94

Frontis: *Orthogonal Space Vectors,* installation, 1990.

CONTENTS

This volume is above all an expression of my deep admiration and friendship for Valie Export, for her person as well as her art. Her willing assistance and generous support of my research in preparation of this manuscript has enhanced my understanding and clarified many aspects of her work for me; it is my hope that I have not carried this clarity to the point of assertion too many times.

I would like to acknowledge the following for photographs used in this volume: Mel Clay, Damm, Gisela Erlacher, Valie Export, Christian W. Fleischmann, Eva Fritsch, Peter Hassmann, Ingeburg Hausmann, Herman Hendrich, Ludwig Hoffenreich, Monika Hubmann, Jarritz & Raider, D. Kirves, Kurt Lesser, Helmut Praschek, Helmut Richter, Gerhard Rimmel, Werner Schulz, Michael Schuster, Eric Timmerman, and Gertraude Wolfsschwenger. I also thank Ingeburg Hausmann for designing the series logo for Women Artists in Film.

ACKNOWLEDGMENTS   My sincere thanks to Regina Cornwell, Robert Nelson, Kaja Silverman, and Trinh T. Minh-ha for their critical reading and suggestions. Finally, I am grateful to Jamie Owen Daniel for her patience in editing the manuscript with me.

The unusually lavish design and photographic material of this volume was made possible by the support of the Ministry of Education and Art, Vienna, Austria.

IU

The transition from the 1950s to the 1960s was a crossroads at which youthful and usable elements of the intellectual and artistic avant-garde of the first half of this century were transferred to the second. The new decade that was ushered in has been assessed in retrospect "as one of the most tumultuous, creative, and vibrant periods that Western culture has ever seen, certainly rivaling the first decades of the twentieth century in Europe."[1] It also marked a time of relatively easier access for women artists attempting to participate in the creative processes of the epoch. The Austrian filmmaker Valie Export, who had her artistic beginnings in this decade, considers herself very much a part of the avant-garde movements of the first half of this century and their continuation and redefinitions after the Second World War. By way of introduction, I would like to outline some of the shifts, transformations, and developments in several of these movements without claiming general art historical currency or On the contrary, I have selectively highlighted those tendencies that have special relevance to Valie Export's work.

Of all the influential groups and centers of learning that prepared the groundwork for this tremendous explosion in the arts, Black Mountain College in North Carolina was one of the most crucial for the preponderance of American art that made itself felt from the sixties on. While Black Mountain College existed for only twenty-four years, its energetic students and teachers carried its influence to all corners of the United States and especially to New York and San Francisco. In the early years following its foundation by John Andrew Rice in 1933, a large sector of the faculty was recruited from artists and intellectuals fleeing totalitarian regimes in Europe. Until 1949 Black Mountain College "was in many respects the spiritual heir to the Bauhaus. They shared a common experimental and anti-academic spirit, a belief in the social responsibility of education and the arts, and an organization that involved both faculty and students in the decision-making process."[2] Josef Albers's course in design, for example, focused on the limits and possibilities of materials in a practical learning experience rather than on teaching how to simply draw on paper. During the last third of the college's existence, these modernist European principles were blended with the experimental spirit of a new generation of young American artists—Robert Rauschenberg, John Cage, and Merce Cunningham, to name just a few—who were then at the beginning of their careers.

In 1952 Cage staged *Theater Piece No. 1,* subsequently acknowledged as the first "Happening." This experimental performance, in which Cage had each of the performers/participants simply be themselves during certain time brackets, had an enormous impact on American art. Happenings were fully developed in the mid- to late-fifties by Pop artists in New York and, in turn, powerfully influenced European artists in the sixties. When Allan Kaprow gave the term "Happening" art historical currency in his famous essay "The Legacy of Jackson Pollock" (1958), he envisioned a bold generation of creators turning garbage and trash into unheard-of artistic events. In many ways Kaprow's inspired predictions for sixties artists were prefigured in Albers's *Werklehre,* which required his students to collect all kinds of odd materials from the city dump. However, the differences in this new generation of American artists are striking. Pollock, and after Pollock, the Happening artists added an automatic approach to making art that became the ruling principle of their production. Although first advocated by the Surrealists, the automatic creation process, as Kaprow sees it, was never wholeheartedly embraced by them. Rather, Kaprow regards the aura that surrounded Happenings as imbued with a sense of ritual and magic that goes back to the beginnings of Western art. From the direct impact of Pollock's paintings, to the environments created by Pop artists, to Kaprow's performance of *18 Happenings in Six Parts,* the progression is unbroken. Despite all the differences, the guiding principle, tracing back to the avant-gardes of the first part of this century, is a concern with the material basis of art, which signalled an abiding interest in the reintegration of life into art and art into life. This interest gained momentum and reached a point of carnal saturation in Viennese Actionism in the mid-sixties. The Viennese Actionists in particular are heirs of the trend in twentieth-century art that developed from a concern with the materiality of the art object, to the belief that "a work of art ought to be a thing added to the world of things rather than a reflection of things that already exist,"[3] to the identification of the human body as the art object par excellence.

Fluxus is another major avant-garde movement that left its imprint on the second part of this century. Closely related to Pop Art and Happenings, it nevertheless claims different antecedents and somewhat different priorities. Fluxus first appeared in print in 1962 as the name of a new art movement in George Maciunas's *Brochure Prospectus for Fluxus Yearbooks,* distributed at a garden party at the Galerie Parnass in Wuppertal, Germany. On that occasion Maciunas also gave a lecture titled "Neo-Dada in the United States," in which he delineated in manifesto fashion the characteristics of the new movement. As the title indicates, Fluxus was viewed as a renewal of Dadaism. Like Dadaism, Fluxus is anti-art, favoring spontaneous, improvised actions over intentionality and the concrete and living over the artistic: "The anti-art forms are primarily directed against art as a profession, against the artificial separation of producer or performer, of generator and spectator or against the separation of art and life."[4] Likewise, with respect to genre distinctions in art, Fluxus sees itself as bridging and frequently merging all forms of art—temporal, spatial, and literary—with music in a dominant position.

An additional similarity to Dada, in this case the Berlin Dada of George Grosz and the Heartfields, is the Fluxus movement's political engagement and antiauthoritarian stance in the wake of McCarthyism and the conservative politics that culminated in the United States's involvement in the Vietnam War. In a 1963 letter to Emmett Williams, George Maciunas wrote: "I know how you feel about involving Fluxus politically with the party (you know which one). Our activities lose all significance if divorced from sociopolitical struggle going on now. We must coordinate our activities or we shall become another 'new wave,' another dada club, coming and going."[5] Fluxus accordingly aligned itself with the major political movements of the sixties, with free speech, Third World liberation, and antiwar protests, collectively referred to as the "student movement."

The Fluxus alignment with these sociopolitical struggles, which led to the revolutionary events in Paris in May 1968, was most thoroughly adopted by the Situationists. An international organization that had developed out of the left wing of the Lettrist movement, the Situationists were strongly based in France. Their contributions survive mainly in the form of theoretical tracts of a rather polemical nature, the sacrosanct center of which are the teachings of Marx and Mao. However, the Situationist notion of revolution as festival is, in its sheer anarchic energy, consonant with the field of energy of that decade.

This brief sketch of some currents in the arts represents the necessary background and reference for the work of Valie Export. Many of the ingredients of these major movements are indispensable for a fuller understanding of Export's work: attention to materials and objects; random selection; spontaneous actions; the elimination of binding categories and formal boundaries between various media, as well as between art and life; and an antiauthoritarian stance on sociopolitical and cultural questions that includes a critical view of the cultural apparatus. Although she is internationally known primarily for her feature films and her performances, Export's artistic beginnings are strongly embedded in the experimental and avant-garde practices of the 1960s. And it would seem that even her feature films cannot be entirely comprehended—this is particularly true of her first feature, *Unsichtbare Gegner* (Invisible Adversaries, 1975–76)—without an awareness of relatively recent currents in art.

While not necessarily more important than international ones, local influences nevertheless offered a more direct insight and access to the young artist and helped define, even if by contrast, her own course of actions. *Die Wiener Gruppe* (the Vienna Group; Achleitner, Artmann, Bayer, Rühm, Wiener) developed in 1952 out of a larger group of progressive artists in Vienna who hoped to reestablish a link with the prewar avant-gardes. In their collaborative efforts, which lasted until 1964, the cohesiveness of the Wiener Gruppe defined itself in terms of their interest in and disputes about language in all of its functions, both theoretical and literary. Wittgenstein was discussed with as much enthusiasm as Gertrude Stein. Their work consisted of sound and concrete poetry, text montages, dramas, radio plays, and chansons. Theoretically, their positions ranged from functionalist overemphasis of language as a tool for social change to an extreme skepticism toward language as an arbitrary limitation to all expressive human capacities on the other. The group's joint work culminated in two literary cabarets, Happening-like performances of their poetic texts that were clearly indebted to Dada.

The dissolution of the group coincided with the formation of what later became known as *Wiener Aktionisten* (Viennese Actionists), another distinct group that included Gunther Brus, Otto Muehl, Hermann Nitsch, and Schwarzkogler. They are not to be confused with the general category *Wiener Aktionismus* (Viennese Actionism), at the outskirts of which Valie Export and other artists and filmmakers developed and expanded their ideas. Oswald Wiener of the Wiener Gruppe, which is also considered part of the larger category of Viennese Actionism, once contrasted his position on questions of language and culture to that of the Actionists, in particular that of Hermann Nitsch. In opposition to Nitsch's belief that "we should have to operate outside the discipline of language in order to replace human communication with actual reality. . . . Reality would begin where language ceases,"[6] Wiener contends that "culture does not obscure reality, it produces it. It is one and the same thing."[7] These differences lead Wiener to wonder why he, nevertheless, considers Nitsch a close associate. He resolves this dilemma by asserting their friendship and at the same time their cultural communality when he writes: "We are party friends, we pursue the same policy of experience: we demand for different reasons the same measure."[8]

The relation between the Viennese Actionists and Happening artists in other countries is evident in terms of format. Both Actionists and Happening artists base themselves on action painting and extend it into three dimensional space, making the spontaneous execution of a prescribed action the focus of the event. However, the Viennese version of Happenings seems in many ways more virulent than, for example, Kaprow's work. The American artist's effort is often seen as a reaction to Abstract Expressionism and "as an attempt on the part of painters to reintroduce recognizable, human content. . . ."[9] Otto Muehl's description of *Materialaktionen* in 1965 as "performed painting" or "autotherapy made visible,"[10] as well as his emphasis on dream processes and associations, direct actions, and the interchangeability of art and life, is very close to the conception and definition of Happenings. However, the taboo-breaking aggressiveness specific to the Actionists is apparent in a 1966 fragment characterizing direct action as "throwing the dirt into people's faces, spoiling art for them . . . no more eroticism . . . instead anti-pornography, chopped off genitals, bloody ears . . ."[11] A long list of intentionally repugnant and gruesome actions follows, concentrating on mutilation of the body and its depiction as merely one primary material among many others. Muehl's sociological context for attacking every cultural value imaginable is elevated into the realm of ritual and myth in Nitsch's *Manifest das lamm* (The Lamb Manifesto), published in conjunction with the 1964 Biennale in Venice. Reminiscent of Artaud's "Theater of Cruelty," Nitsch's *Orgien Mysterien Theater* (Orgies Mysteries Theatre, or simply, "o.m. theater"), a six-day festival, was an attempt to return to the deepest layers of drama, locating it, as did Nietzsche, in the early Greek cult of Dionysus. According to Nitsch, in Christian mythology the rite of Dionysus is transformed into the death of the lamb of

God on the cross, which corresponds to a deep-seated desire of the collective human psyche for sensual excess, cruelty, and finally catharsis. "The obscene bloody intoxication of these pictures," writes Peter Gorsen, "does not aim at a further soiling or defiling, but is the neurotic cipher for the purification and renewal of civilization."[12]

These are some of the main characteristics of the immediate artistic climate at the beginning of Valie Export's career. Her personal acquaintance with the Actionists and her frequent attendance of their events allowed for ample exposure to their ideas, which she subsequently transformed but which are still recognizable in her early body actions, such as those captured on the two expanded movies *Cutting* (1967–68) and *Genitalpanik* (Genital Panic, 1969). What connected Export's work in the sixties and early seventies with Viennese Actionism was her proclivity toward breaking social, sexual, and cultural taboos and her predilection for the human body as the principal material in her work. What distinguished her from the Actionists definitively from the very beginning was her inclusion of technology in her work and, more importantly, her transformation of the Actionists' use of the female body. In accordance with the sexual politics of the day, women's bodies were primarily passive objects to be acted upon rather than actors in their own right. The packaged, smeared, used, and abused bodies of women were central to some Actionist fantasies of destruction. And it is precisely this aspect that rendered their rebellion instantly obsolete, as women began to formulate their own protests, protests whose target was the kind of objectification of women essential to Actionist practice. In contrast, Export's early actions with Peter Weibel, while not explicitly feminist in their conception, can at least be considered a step in that direction in as far as they assign active, even dominant roles to the woman. In the 1969 *Kriegkunstfeldzug* (Martial Arts Campaign) and action performed in Munich, Cologne, Zurich, and Essen within the context of the multimedia program "underground explosion," Export whipped the audience as Weibel sprayed them with water using high-pressure hoses. In the 1968 action *Aus der Mappe der Hundigkeit* (From the Portfolio of Doggedness), Export leads Weibel on all fours on a leash through a busy downtown section of Vienna. Their official explanation was to "proclaim the negative utopia of erect posture in our animalistic society." Although her dominant role is not mentioned as an important ingredient of the action, when seen against the background of Viennese Actionism, it is nonetheless strikingly refreshing in its reversal of the usual distribution of positions. While not articulated as feminist, the role assigned to women in these artistic events of the sixties places Export into a category of her own.

A different treatment of the body went hand in hand with the upgrading of women's roles. The Actionists' conception was sculptural, placing the body into space as a three-dimensional object and making it subject to destruction along with all other objects and materials. Export, recognizing the reductionist tendencies in their unilateral demolition actions, developed a concept of the body as expansive. Taking it out of the static realm of objectification, Export releases the body into the mobility of signifying interrelations. The body embedded in and part of a system of communication is neither identical with this system nor immune to it. It is affected by all the factors that go into defining a particular social and cultural environment, upon which it, in turn, exerts its influence through psychosomatic givens. While this dialectic exchange between body and culture is most evident in Export's performances, it is one of the major concerns of all of her art. This expansive view of the body also places much importance on the use of different media, and it is not surprising that Export's work, in contrast to that of the Viennese Actionists, not only included, but emphasized technological media like film and video from the outset.

VALIE EXPORT

FRAGMENTS OF THE IMAGINATION

1

Expanded Cinema

Export's experimental work in the 1960s consists predominantly of expanded movies. This group of actions or film shorts is characterized by their investigation of film as material and process. These concerns were in line not only with independent filmmakers in the United States and in other countries but also with larger avant-garde developments in the arts. "Like the tendency exhibited in painting and the other arts, recent filmmakers have chosen modes of reduction of the technical-formal options available to them. Their work asks what film is and what its irreducible elements are."[1] More specifically, the term "Expanded Cinema" is closely related, as Birgit Hein explains in *Film as Film,* to the whole movement of Expanded Arts, which explored and experimented with multimedia events and Happenings. At that time one of the common ways to define art was in terms of correspondences between various disciplines: "Our time demands that art be a system of correspondences, within which each unit is developed to such a degree that it touches on other systems, those of topology for example, or of crystallography, of sociometry, plasmaphysics, nuclear chemistry or molecular biology."[2] Yet it was not only the crossover between various disciplines, categories, and genres that was at stake, but also the general tendency, begun by the classical avant-gardes at the beginning of this century, to break through all confinements imposed upon the definition and the practice of art: "If we can understand how painters, after 'Action Painting,' needed to move the action beyond the canvas, then we can also understand the urge of film-makers to move the frame beyond the screen."[3]

Discernible within the framework of these general tendencies are a number of differing directions that result from divergent emphases. The expansion of consciousness described by Gene Youngblood as "man's ongoing historical drive to manifest his consciousness outside of his mind, in front of his eyes"[4] was in its most general sense also a goal of Expanded Cinema. In the course of the sixties, however, the emphasis on consciousness expansion became increasingly identified with countercultural Happenings characterized by drug experiences and light shows. Other directions continued the experiments of the formal and political avant-gardes of the twenties. Like their predecessors, these artists concerned themselves with exploring the possibilities of the medium beyond the simple projection of a filmstrip onto the screen, as well as with investigating the question of ownership of the means of artistic production and its impact on the structure of communication. They advocated greater interaction between art and the public—not in the sense of the public as mass culture but in terms of greater accessibility of public institutions to the individual artist. This demanded scrutiny of all facets of the cultural apparatus, including the audience, much as Brecht and Benjamin had done in the twenties. Fluxus reinforced these tendencies with its combination of directly political concerns and the investigation of the fundamentals of the medium. Valie Export has acknowledged the importance of Fluxus on her early work. And further, she supports Birgit Hein's assessment of Expanded Cinema as an "aspect of structural film."[5] Export has located Expanded Cinema under the double determination of the revolts of the student movement that waged an attack against dominant oppressive state power, and . . . the artistic developments of this period that sought a new definition of the concept of art. Its aesthetic was aimed at making people aware of refinements and shifts of sensibility, the structures and conditions of visual and emotional communication, so as to render our amputated sense of perception capable of perception again.[6]

Her mention of "sensibility" and "perception" echoes the general concern of the period with the expansion of consciousness, but Export's particular concern is quite firmly embedded in the rigor of her artistic practice, as well as in a keen understanding of the politics in this practice.

Within this framework of intertextual expansiveness, Export privileges materiality and the body. This principle is expressed in various ways: either by exploring and possibly substituting film materials (screen, projector, etc.) with other analogous processes and materials (e.g., a mirror as projector-reflector), or by focussing on the interaction/reception situation of film and on the actors/audience. A third and more extreme possibility is the use of the human body (actor/audience) as film material. This last category approaches Export's later body performances. Pieces such as *Touch Cinema* or *Genitalpanik,* for example, which are concerned with the ideological effect of cinema, exclusively take the human body for their material. Generally, the lack of hard-and-fast criteria for assigning these experimental works to certain categories, as well as the fluidity of their form and content, must be kept in mind in this attempt to give an overview of Export's prolific output in the sixties.

In the attempt to replace ordinary film materials (such as projector, screen, and the filmstrip itself) the film *Abstract Film No. 1* (1967–68), with the subtitle "light–land–water–mirror action," minimizes technology as far as possible. In this experiment, a bright spotlight is held over a mirror that is doused with various liquids. Abstract patterns are produced and then reflected onto a screen. The screen itself can be replaced by natural features such as rocks, trees, etc. This reduction to

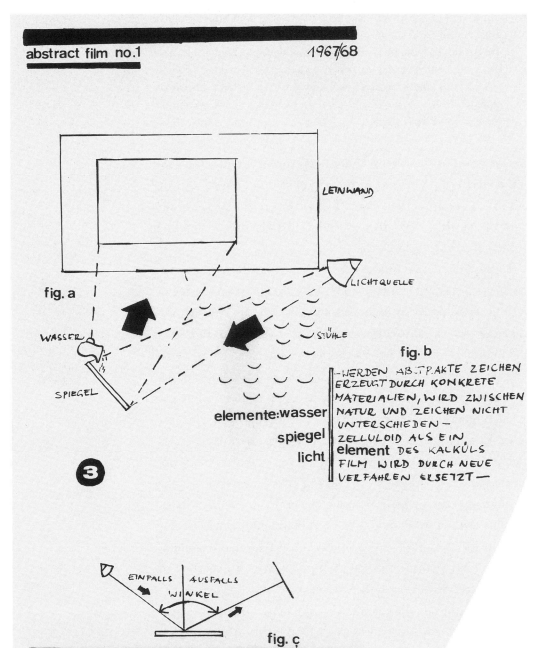

Abstract Film No. 1, 1967–68.

Abstract Film No. 1.

simpler, often natural elements was intended as an antitechno-
logical gesture, as Export confirmed in her commentary on the
film: "The recourse to natural means such as water and simple
reflection, the reduction to separate elements, the turning away
from technology create unexpected but basically understand-
able relations to land art, minimal art and art povera."[7] The
border crossing between nature and culture, life and art so crucial to the definition of Expanded Cinema is perfectly represented in this piece.

Ars Lucis (1967–68), a mirror-and-screen environment,
derives its effects entirely from such artifacts as projectors, film-
strips, cylindrical prisms, solid and moveable mirrors, and
curved screens used as projection surfaces in addition to the
walls and ceiling of the performance area. Film projectors
on rotating discs, whose images are periodically intercepted,

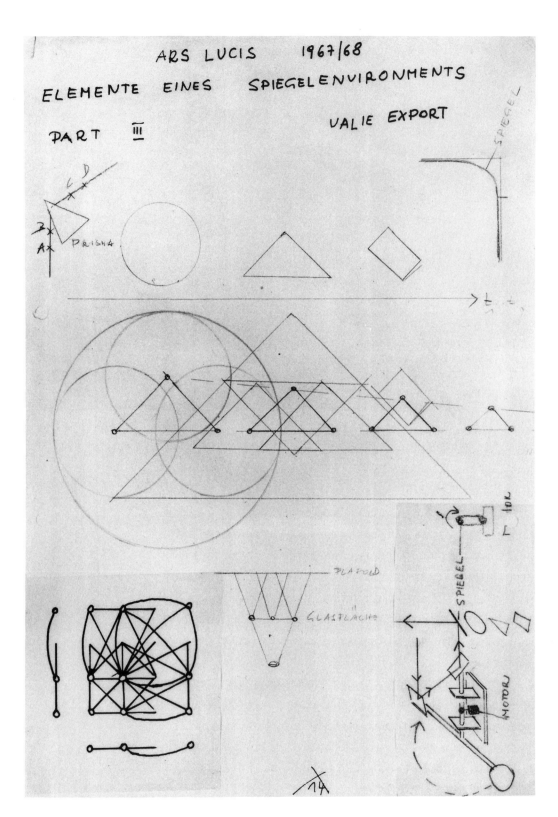

Ars Lucis, 1967–68.

distorted, and fractured by the prisms, cover the entire environment with their reflections.[8] Here the expansion happens through complete immersion, the total integration of the participants/ spectators in a space turned into a work of art by way of a complex relay of mirrors, prisms, and film images. There is an interactive dimension to *Ars Lucis* in one further feature of the environment: light-sensitive cells are installed in a few places to trigger additional movement of the projectors and screens as a result of the participants' walking around and creating a light/dark (shadow) pattern picked up by the cells.[9]

Another environment film *Ohne Titel xn* (Without Title xn, 1968), involves very large three-dimensional objects placed into spaces in which the audience/participants can walk around. Films projected into this environment alter its ambience periodically, from skies, to water, to city traffic, and so on. The total immersion of the participants/audience in these environment films is an important aspect of Expanded Cinema as conceived by Export. In one of her commentaries on that period, she writes that Expanded Cinema developed under the aegis of "total art, which annuls the borders between artificial and natural reality, between given and possible reality, between products and producers, between humans and objects."[10]

While participants are fairly passive in the environment films, other expanded movies such as *Instant Film* (1968) and *Das magische Auge* (The Magic Eye, 1969), both made in collaboration with Peter Weibel, emphasize the breakdown between production and consumption. Their goal is to shake spectators out of their consumers' lethargy and oblige them to participate actively. *Instant Film,* whose title humorously refers to the myriad instant objects and foods on the market, consists of nothing but a sheet of see-through plastic. The participants can take it home and produce their own film out of their own reality, not by projecting anything onto the material but by looking through it. The sheet can be prepared in various ways by cutting, coloring, etc., and becomes the projector, the screen, and the film_strip all in one. *Instant Film* is also called an "object film," offering itself to be used as an object. Weibel and Export wrote the following text to accompany the piece in 1968:

> *Instant Film* is a meta-film that reflects the system of film and reality. After the development of instant coffee and instant milk, we have finally succeeded in inventing the "instant film," which is screen, projector and camera in one. Assembling them is a matter for the viewer. He can hang the foil at home on his own four walls, on four screens, or on different colored backgrounds, he can place the foil in front of an object and in such a way design his own collage. A foil which has been prepared with scissors, cigarettes, etc., supplies at any given moment "vistas" or "insights," "views" directed inward or outward.[11]

By comparison, *The Magic Eye* is far more complex and involves an electronically prepared screen and light-sensitive cells. The

The Magic Eye, 1969.

screen, again made of plastic, transposes the differences in the quality of light, caused either by the shadows of the audience or of a filmstrip, into sounds. It is "the world's first autogenerative sound screen, a true sound picture."[12] In his discussion of *The Magic Eye,* Malcolm Le Grice argues that the "intention is not simply to create sound from light, but to demonstrate how information can be divorced from specific semantic implications and instead seen as a physical, material problem."[13]

By involving the audience as actors, whether demonstrational or creative, critical, and active, these expanded movies approximate performance pieces. As long as the filmic process as such is central, however, they are best defined as interactive Expanded Cinema. It might be useful, however, to distinguish between the more passive interaction of the audience in its simple immersion in an environment and the active interaction in pieces that consciously critique the very passivity of total immersion. *Ping Pong* (1968) is perhaps the most interesting experiment in this category, as it illustrates in comic fashion the structural deficiencies of the cinematic viewing situation. An actor (representing the audience) stands in front of the screen equipped with Ping-Pong ball and paddle. The film projected onto the screen consists only of dots, slowly appearing and disappearing in different places, depicting targets the player tries to hit. The structural relation between screen and audience is thus characterized as one of stimulus and reaction, whereby the screen, i.e., the film director, makes the decisions and the audience follows passively. This film was chosen as the "most political film" at the Viennese Film Festival in November 1968 (2d Maraisiade). This label is not surprising in the context of film-theoretical debates of the sixties, which were strongly influenced by Brecht's notion of the apparatus as a field of signification encompassing the technical tools proper, as well as the cultural institutions and the parties in control of those institutions. On the basis of this nexus of meanings, the demonstrative structural subordination of the spectator to the authority of the spectacle can easily be seen as political intervention.

Ping Pong, 1968.

A remedy to this unsatisfactory situation is suggested in *Auf+Ab+An+Zu* (Up+Down+On+Off, 1968). A filmstrip of a statue in an encircling 360° view is partially painted over in geometric patterns that block some of the outlines. The strip is then projected onto a paper screen. The actor/participant stationed in front of the screen completes the missing lines by drawing directly on the paper screen. As the filmstrip is three minutes long, the completing lines are superimposed in montage fashion, resulting in a painting that exists in its own right at the end. Export called this film a *"Lehrfilm"* (learning film) in reference to Brecht's *"Lehrstück"* (learning play), which also aimed to eliminate the distinction between actor and audience in an effort to do away with the traditional division in theater between active, creative producers and passively receptive audiences. Confronting the usual filmic sequencing (from shooting to montage to projection) with the simultaneity of montage and

Up+Down+On+Off, 1968.

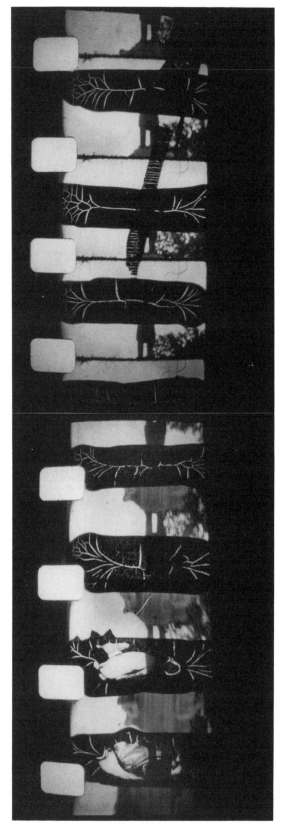

Up+Down+On+Off.

projection "robs the producers of their conventional success," because "sabotaging the time structure (of the production scheme) means that 'reality' is no longer fabricated, rather, the possibility of fabricating 'reality' is demonstrated."[14]

Split Screen–Solipsismus (1968) is set in counterpoint to the idea of film as psychological crutch, exemplified by *Ansprache Aussprache* (Address Redress, 1968). *Split Screen–Solipsismus*, which takes its cue from Vertov (who liked to be filmed at the edge of store windows), works with illusion-creating effects, in this case the doubling of the image by means of reflection. A mirror or a piece of foil is placed at an angle to the screen. The image of a boxer hitting a punching ball is projected onto the screen in such a way that the ball is at the edge of the frame. The mirror, however, creates the effect of the boxer fighting himself. In contrast to this meditation on the formal capacities of film to

Split Screen–Solipsismus, 1968.

Address Redress, 1968.

create doubles, superimpositions, and copies in its technological procedures, *Address Redress* explores the psychological power of film. An image of a cheering and clapping crowd is projected onto a transparent plastic screen. The actor in front of the screen gives a speech, voices complaints, or whatever, and is assured of applause. The text accompanying this performance recommends undergoing the procedure as an ego booster before exams, conferences, and similar anxiety-producing events. Both pieces are highly ironic in their titles. *Split Screen–Solipsismus* in particular points to film as a source of psychic disorders. Splitting, according to Freud, occurs as a result of the fetish defense in the oedipal conflict, which Christian Metz has described as the preferred structure of Hollywood film; solipsism reflects the isolation of the viewing situation. *Address Redress*, on the other hand, hints at the potential for film, and the mass media for that matter, to become an instrument of demagoguery.

However much European Expanded Cinema privileged political-theoretical considerations, its practitioners made occasional excursions into countercultural investigations related to the sixties' interest in drug-induced perceptions. *Der Kuss* (The Kiss, 1968) and *Ohne Titel Nr. 2* (Without Title No. 2, 1968), both made in collaboration with Peter Weibel, are attempts to parallel through purely filmic means the effects of drugs on vision. Techniques such as slow motion, superimpositions, associations, etc. attempted to imitate certain states of mind "expansion."

In the final group of expanded movies, the actors' bodies substitute in one way or another for the film materials. In most pieces, the focus is on breaking sexual taboos with the intent to prevent the commercial exploitation of the taboos. Most notorious among these expanded films are *Tapp und Tastkino* (Touch Cinema, 1968) and *Genitalpanik* (Genital Panic, 1969). Both of them take up the question of voyeurism in the movies, the fact that the film spectator's interest is locked in through the promise of disclosure of the forbidden. In the majority of commercial films the forbidden revolves around the body of woman, more specifically her breasts and genitals. In *Touch Cinema* the

Touch Cinema, 1968.

voyeurism is undercut by reversing the cinematic viewing situation. Instead of being able to hide in a dark room, anonymously engaged in spurious pleasure, the spectator is encouraged to enjoy the "real thing"—but out in the open, in the middle of the street, where he can be seen by everybody. For this purpose

VALIE EXPORT

Touch Cinema.

Export strapped a mini–movie theater (plastic or metal box with curtains) over her bare chest while Peter Weibel exhorted the passersby to participate. The tenor of the sixties' emphasis on sexual liberation is evident, but what is not so obvious is that Export also considered it a "true woman's film." She describes it as "woman's first step from object to subject. She disposes of her breasts freely and no longer follows social prescriptions; the fact that everything happens in the street and the 'consumer' can be anybody, i.e., man or woman, constitutes an undisguised infraction of the homosexuality taboo."[15] *Genital Panic* works with the same principle of accessibility, only this time inside the cinema, as Export, with the front of her pants cut out, walks through the rows of spectators. To combat voyeurism in the cinema through greater bodily accessibility no longer seems viable twenty years later; it does represent, however, the first steps away from male-dominated sexual liberation and toward a feminist insistence on the control over one's own body.

Genital Panic, 1969.

Cutting (1967–68), the first film by Export to use the body as film material, is a McLuhanesque meditation on the assertion that "the content of writing is speech." Cutting as film-technical operation is here given a determining role in the creation of film reality, which is not seen in opposition to reality as such. An attempt is made to transfer the act of cutting to aspects of film other than the filmstrip. Thus, in one of its five parts, entitled "opening, a documentary," a paper screen on which a window is being projected is literally cut open. And in another move of substitution and punning literalness, the technical term "body cutter" finds its interpretation in the shaving (cutting) of the torso of a man to be used as the screen. Some of these film-technical deliberations and substitutions take on a strictly hypothetical character as they explore areas of the human body that cannot be dealt with in the prescribed way without serious injury. *Tonfilm* (Sound Film, 1969) and *Proselyt* (Proselyte, 1969) fall into this category. *Sound Film* provides for the operation of a photoelectric amplifier in the glottis, connected to a light-sensitive resistor placed on the outside of the face. The amplifier regulates the voice's volume depending on the amount of light or dark outside. *Proselyte* proposes the destruction of the spectator's fovea centralis in the retina through the emission of rays coming from the screen. After the capacity to distinguish colors has thus been eliminated, the spectator can begin "to see the truth in black and white . . . the loss of bright red sunsets over blue oceans is compensated for by a simplification of the vocabulary, a better overview over the environment and an increase in the defence against illusions. . . . "[16] This sarcastic dystopia is subtitled *1989,* possibly one-upping *1984.* In the last film of this category, *Adjungierte Dislokationen* (Adjoined Dislocations, 1973), the body acts as a kind of tripod. Two 8mm cameras are tied to the front and the back of the upper part of the torso, taking simultaneous pictures in opposite directions. If the body bends down, for example, the frontal camera takes images of the street while the camera on the back films the sky. This action was itself filmed with a

Cutting, 1967–68.

Cutting.

Cutting.

Cutting.

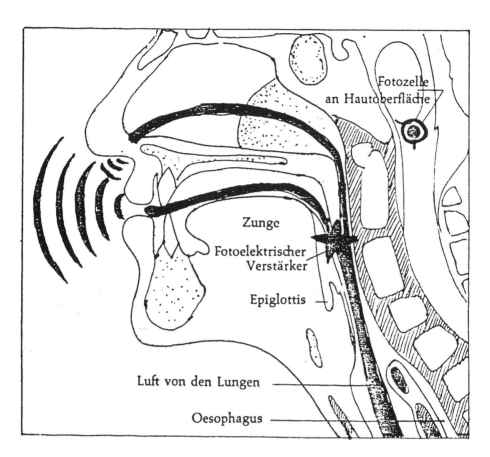

Fotozelle
an Hautoberfläche

Zunge

Fotoelektrischer
Verstärker

Epiglottis

Luft von den Lungen

Oesophagus

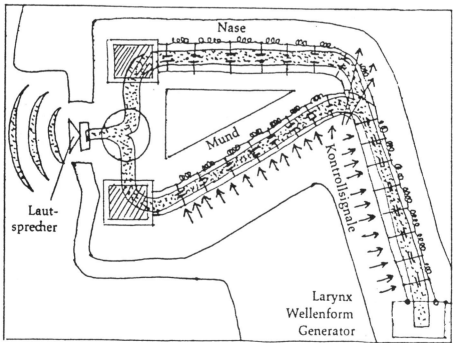

Nase

Mund

Kontrollsignale

Laut-
sprecher

Larynx
Wellenform
Generator

Sound Film, 1969.

16mm camera. The final projection showed the 16mm side by side with the two 8mm films. In this way "what is demonstrated is not only the investigation of the environment on film but a film of the investigation of the environment through the body, which turns the environment into a body, into the body's extension, into an environmental body."[17] As the last in a diverse series of expanded movies, *Adjoined Dislocations* coincides with the high point of Export's performance art, an important segment of which dealt precisely with the body and its relation to the environment.

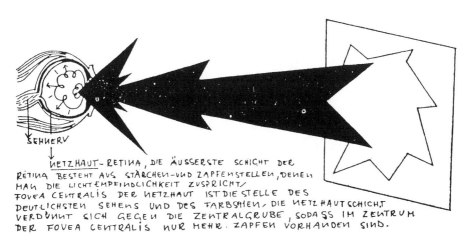

SEHNERV

NETZHAUT- RETINA, DIE ÄUSSERSTE SCHICHT DER RETINA BESTEHT AUS STÄBCHEN- UND ZAPFENSTELLEN, DENEN MAN DIE LICHTEMPFINDLICHKEIT ZUSPRICHT/ FOVEA CENTRALIS DER NETZHAUT IST DIE STELLE DES DEUTLICHSTEN SEHENS UND DES FARBSEHEN, DIE NETZHAUTSCHICHT VERDÜNNT SICH GEGEN DIE ZENTRALGRUBE, SODASS IM ZENTRUM DER FOVEA CENTRALIS NUR MEHR ZAPFEN VORHANDEN SIND.

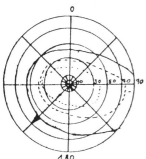

DURCH RETINALSTRAHLUNG WERDEN DIE DURCH DIE FARBIGEN LICHTER ERREGBAREN SUBSTANZEN ZERSTÖRT/ ES BLEIBT SOMIT DANN NUR MEHR DIE SCHWARZ-WEISSE SUBSTANZ ÜBER, DIE AUSSENWELT ERSCHEINT GLEICH EINER SCHWARZ-WEISS FOTOGRAPHIE/

GESICHTSFELD DES AUGES GRENZEN FÜR WEISSES LICHT= ——— FÜR BLAU U GELB - — — , FÜR ROT U. GRÜN = = ... (NACH ABDERHALDEN)

Proselyte, 1969.

Adjoined Dislocations, 1973.

Adjoined Dislocations.

2

Performances—Actions—Video— Installations

Performances/Actions

It becomes extremely difficult to distinguish between the various art forms included under the rubric of Expanded Art. Expanded Cinema is relatively easy to isolate because of its distinct concern with the materials and processes of cinema. However, establishing hard-and-fast criteria that separate action painting from performance, or performance from dance, theater, or music becomes a difficult task[1] that is best not attempted in the first place: the fusion into "intermedia," as Dick Higgins has named this process of hybridization, was one of the most significant characteristics of art after 1958. What is interesting about Higgins's description of intermedia is not only his insistence that they represent a conceptual fusion rather than a simple mixing, but also that they coincide with the dissolution of the individual artist's grand narrative: "the artist ceases to create his own myth (as he had been doing, typically, since the mid-nineteenth century)."[2] This move away from the artist's search for coherent self-representation coincides with a greater emphasis on the working materials, not as an avoidance of emotion but, as Higgins put it, as an "unwillingness to impose oneself needlessly on the materials with which one is working."[3] And from this shift of paradigms he derives the "distinction between *acting,* in the old art, and *enacting* in the new art . . . today we enact our rituals of performance, stressing the materials of performance more than our own identities."[4]

In his 1968 essay "The Death of the Author," Roland Barthes describes the author as a product of Western societies dependent on the notion of the individual as it developed from the Middle Ages to the Reformation, culminating in bourgeois, capitalist ideology. When Barthes proposes that at the moment "the author enters into his own death, writing begins,"[5] he points to very much the same phenomenon of attention to the working material at hand rather than to the identity of the artist. This is also the case when he locates the practice of "writing" not only in various modernist and avant-garde modes, but also in the "performance" of narratives in "ethnographic societies," where the performer is a "mediator, a shaman or relator"[6] who masters the narrative code instead of being considered a "genius."

Some interesting inferences for modern performance art can be drawn from these observations. Beyond the obliteration of the operation of recording and representation that follows placing the emphasis entirely on the *hic et nunc* of the act of performance, another consideration emerges. Performance as "enactment" or "writing" can accommodate the margin. As the individuality of the author is no longer central to the creative process, members of groups whose specific subject position had hitherto prevented them from participating in the production of art are now enabled to join. Although Barthes did not elaborate on this directly, the fact that he chose Mallarmé and Proust as precursors of "writing" probably had less to do with their modernist practice than with their personal marginality. Likewise, Surrealism was chosen to represent the avant-garde for its exploration of the unconscious as well as its communal writing practice, despite its inability "to accord language a supreme place."[7] In moving away from the consciousness of the individual artist and toward materiality, those who have been deprived of history and of subjecthood finally have a chance to engage in artistic endeavor.

This aspect of performance could also partly explain why almost half of the performances of the seventies were given by women, a surprising percentage given the fact that in the early sixties, women were "still very much in the minority among Activists and Happeningists."[8] One obvious explanation for these statistics can be found in the lack of conventions and traditions which make performance art more accessible to women. This view is, of course, related to the notion that performance is inclusive of the margin, yet it falls short of an aesthetic explanation. In her definition of Feminist Actionism,[9] Export comes much closer to seeing the accessibility of performance to women in terms of its aesthetic strategies, strategies not unlike those of "writing" and "enacting":

> Just as action aims at achieving the unity of actor and material, perception and action, subject and object, Feminist Actionism seeks to transform the object of male natural history, the material "woman," subjugated and enslaved by the male creator, into an independent actor and creator, object of her own history. For without the ability to express oneself and without a field of action, there can be no human dignity.[10]

Through their identification with materiality and objects, women are drawn into this unity of doing and being in performance. For Higgins, the unity was achieved on the basis of a renunciation of identity in favor of the material; women performers arrived at this position from the opposite angle, by searching for subjecthood. In other words, for the male artist the subject/object unity in performance was achieved by letting go his overriding concern with his own subjectivity in favor of the object and of materiality, whereas for women the question posed itself in terms of a gain in subjecthood to counteract their overdetermined object status. "Enacting" for women artists would therefore not signify so much a shift in favor of materiality as a shift toward "enabling" them to act.

While Feminist Actionism had many antecedents—Action Painting, Happenings, Action Art, Fluxus, and much earlier, Dada—it is Surrealism, Tachism, and Art Informel that Export mentions most emphatically, and for the same reasons that Barthes had singled out Surrealism in his notion of "writing": its techniques of articulating the repressed and the unconscious. The significance of this emphasis derives from what Export has called "the primary source" of Feminist Actionism, which she believes to be "the history of female experience."[11] Memory provides a kind of history, not only of the repressed individual psyche, but also of the history of the dark continent of female repression. It is this aspect of the unconscious that informs Export's performance and body work of the seventies, as well as her definition of Feminist Actionism. Her roll call of women's names, from Dorothy Wordsworth to Sylvia Plath, reads like the history of female existences, talent, and artistic careers thwarted under the sway of patriarchal jurisdiction. Feminist Actionism exposes these experiences as

> historical scars, traces of ideas inscribed onto the body, stigmata to be exposed by actions with the body. If they are interpreted as pathologies of self-hatred, poor self-esteem, sorrow, subjugation, or even identification with the oppressor, then they are part of the truth of women's history. And the myth is such that only very few women are ready to scrape away the veneer. Many prefer the illusion of meaningless glamour to the sovereignty of fully exposed pain and to the *painful energy of resistance*.[12]

While most of her videotapes and installations in the seventies were structural explorations of the possibilities of the new medium for artistic purposes, the testing ground of Feminist Actionism must be sought in Export's work involving the body. Most of this work consists of performances and actions, actions being distinguished from performances in their randomness with respect to audience. The spectators at an action, in other words, are not invited for a particular event but are casually confronted with the action in their everyday life-context. While performance still maintains the concept of the stage in materials and presentation, actions try to dispense with this whole complex and instead utilize public space and simple means of expression. The break between the structural explorations of Export's video work, including her expanded movies and the more visceral experiments of her body work, should not be exaggerated, since on the one hand technology is explored as material, and on the other, the body is treated as sign and system of codes. Export explains: "I have also found a way to continue expanded cinema in my physical performances in which I, as the center point for the performance, positioned the human body as a sign, as a code for social and artistic expression."[13] It is important to point out in this context that Export's body work does not constitute an apotheosis of the body; rather, it considers the body as one material among many (such as glass, lead, electricity, wax, oil, animals, etc.).

The special appropriateness of body work for feminism must be seen in the equation of woman and body, which is as old as patriarchal society itself. It is also for this reason that all the performances and actions (with the exception of *From the Portfolio of Doggedness*) center on the female body and are demonstrated by the artist herself. Only occasionally is an action or a performance repeated by another woman. From the beginning, the body in Export's work was conceived as the bearer of signs, signals, and information. This designation goes in two directions. On one hand, it means that the body is the site of cultural determinations, the place where the law of society is engraved into the individual. On the other, it also implies the body's capacity to signal to the outside world and communicate with it. The 1968 performance *Fingergedicht* (Finger Poem), subsequently turned into a two-minute videotape entitled *Sehtext* (Visual Text) that became the foundation of Export's serial photography, is the most graphic and literal demonstration of the expressive power of the body. *Body sign action* (1970) is also a powerfully literal example of the other side of the body's sign function: the body as field of inscription by a social code. The text to this action describes the piece as follows: "The photograph shows a tattooed garter

From the Portfolio of Doggedness, 1969.

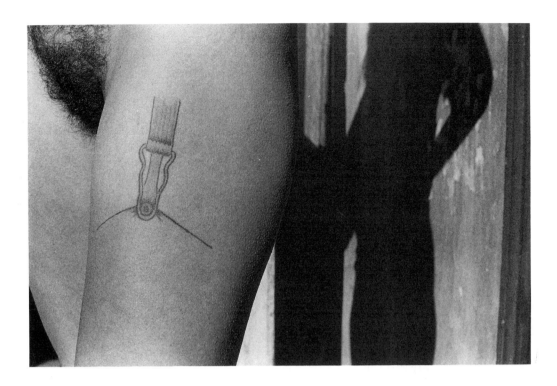

body sign action, 1970.

on my thigh. The garter is used as a sign of past enslavement, as a symbol of repressed sexuality. The garter as the sign of belonging to a class that demands conditioned behavior becomes a reminiscence that keeps awake the problem of self-determination and/or determination by others of femininity."[14] Aside from this very clear explanation, *body sign action* also plays with analogies between the human being and books. Just as the first books were inscribed on animal skins, the skin of the person is inscribed (as in ritual tattooing) and becomes a medium for communication. Books are in this sense only an extension of the human body. However, Export also addresses the body's difference from books and all traditional methods of recording, transmitting, and saving signs for posterity. Since the duration of this artwork is congruent with the existence of the artist, there is no posthumous work.

The recognition that society has such a determining grip on the body instantly entails strategies for counteracting this strangle-

Eros/ion, 1970.

hold, since from a feminist point of view, most of these determinations are not for and by women. In this early stage the body becomes a battlefield on which the struggle for self-determination takes place. The 1971 body–material interaction *Eros/ion* is perhaps the most forceful and also the most shocking example of this battle. The naked performer rolls first through an area strewn with broken glass, then over a plate of glass, and finally onto a paper screen. This movement is repeated several times for approximately ten minutes. Two aspects of this action are of particular importance. First is the notion of "conquering" the body, to continue the terminology of battle. The minor wounds sustained from the broken glass (injuries were minor because the glass used was very thin and tended to move laterally when pressed down) left traces on the paper screen not unlike the traces left by Yves Klein's human paint brushes, although within

Eros/ion.

an entirely self-directed frame. This process of aestheticizing a possibly lethal situation showed the way toward overcoming determination by a given context and redirecting the meaning of that context. In other words, *Eros/ion* is also an exercise in semantics. The body as bearer of self-inflicted signs creates another meaning out of its wounded state. What takes place is a change in context. And this is the other emphasis of the performance: glass, when broken, signifies cutting and pain, and yet when in one piece, as in a window pane, it signifies transparency. Context overrides material. Similarly, the self-imposed engraving of the skin in an aesthetic context could be seen to represent the overcoming of social and cultural imprints (*body sign action* is based on the same notion). *Eros/ion* was performed in 1971 in Frankfurt at the "experimenta 4," in London at the "arts lab," and in Amsterdam at the "electric cinema."

An intensification and elaboration of the thoughts that contributed to *Eros/ion* surfaced in the performance *Kausalgie* (Causalgia, 1973), conceived in four parts. Part one consists of a slide taken from Gregory Bateson's book *Naven*. The slide is called "cutting" and shows an initiation rite in a tribal society. The novice's back is being cut as other members stand by, watching the operation. The slide is accompanied by a text on tape, which reads

> "cutting" shows the body as site of civilization. Just as the body of the animal is branded as somebody's property in the course of the socialization of nature, the human being is embedded in society through the body. The body is marked with social signals, with signs of belonging to gender, tribe, territory, with "protective" formulas, with "persona" formulas. The initiation ritual shows concretely how the human being is fitted into the social mythology and structure through the body.[15]

In the second part of the performance, the artist breaks open the brick wall that had just served as projection surface for the slide. With hammer and chisel she makes a square hole in the wall. Then she cuts open the dress of another woman performer. In the accompanying text, clothes are called the second, and houses the third skin of the body, suggesting that some kind of personal liberation can be achieved through refusing social and institutional regulation and prescription. The third part is another slide, showing the garter tattoo of *body sign action*. Again a taped text is read, which applies the discourse of the first two parts to the question of woman:

> Woman is forced to represent herself through jewelry, make-up, personality and as bearer of fixed sexual symbols which are signs of a phallocratic society, in a way that does not correspond to her personal needs. Based on the system of biological differences, a sociological system of repression was erected, which woman can escape only by rejecting the body defined in this manner as feminine.[16]

Finally, as the text accompanying the fourth part announces, the fourth part demonstrates the painful process that marks the

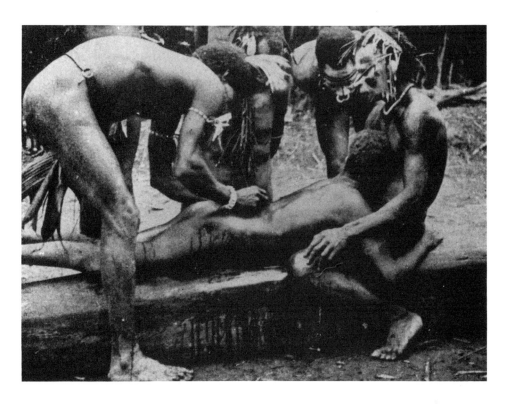

Causalgia, 1973.

Causalgia.

Causalgia.

Causalgia.

Causalgia.

passage from used object to self-determined subject. The shadow of a man standing on a swastika falls onto a wax plate lying on the floor. The stage floor itself is turned into a "verbal scaffolding for the action,"[17] strewn with words that are meant to stimulate associations in the spectators: "order–lack of freedom–freedom–chaos"; "the human being is a medium of communication a bearer of symbols and information." The outline of the shadow is burned into the wax. The woman performer lies down, nude, inside this shadow image as the man begins to surround her with electrical wire connected to a battery. Gradually, the warmth of her body leaves an impression in the wax plate, and the woman's task now is to liberate herself from this imprisonment by rolling across the wire and onto a paper screen. The lack of traces or impressions on the paper may suggest the possibility of independence from external definition. The pain caused by the electric wires is described as "white causalgia," the light pain of liberation, as opposed to "black causalgia," the dark pain of oppression in the shadow realm of the man. At the end of the performance the imprint on the wax plate is covered with liquid lead, putting a lid on the patriarchal image of woman, as it were. *Causalgia* was performed in 1973 at the Galerie Maerz in Linz, Austria, and at the "Steirische Herbst" in Graz.

Closely related to the fourth part of *Causalgia* is the performance *Hyperbulie* (Hyperbulia, also performed by Export in 1973). Once again, limitations and enforced social determinations are illustrated through electrical wires. This time the naked woman performer must pass through a narrow corridor of electrical wires. The frequent contact with the loaded wire decreases strength, so that she finally sinks to the ground. She is only able to leave the enclosure thanks to a near pathological act of will (hyperbulia, the meaning of the title). The reduction of woman to an animal is encoded both in electric wires, used to "pasture" c(h)attle, and in the final posture of the woman performer as she crawls out of the corridor on all fours. The dangerous and narrow passage is also an act of initiation and part of the symbolic formula of myths and legends concerned with enlightenment and transcendence. Here the motif is applied to women's rite of passage out of oppression and toward independence and self-determination.

Asemie (Asemia, 1973; performed in Vienna) is the last in this trilogy of performances whose titles refer to a condition of sickness or pathology. "Causalgia," defined as burning pain caused by an injury to the nervous system, and "Hyperbulia," a

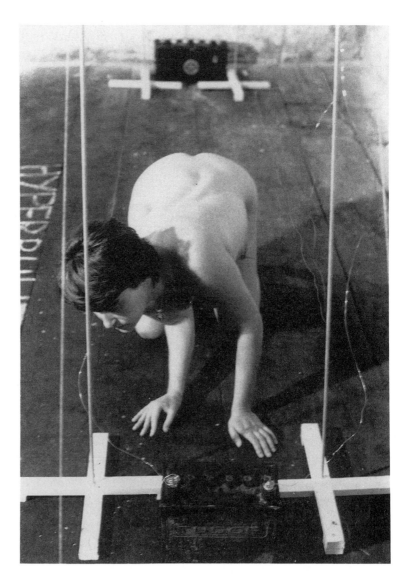

Hyperbulia, 1973.

VALIE EXPORT

 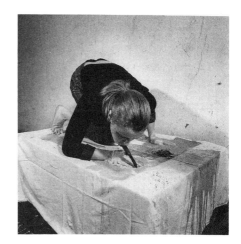

Asemia, 1973.

pathological increase in willpower, both focus on the price paid for breaking out of conventional expectations placed on women. *Asemia* describes what happens when this step is not taken. The subtitle reads, "The inability to express oneself through mimicry." Expressive asemia, a disrupted response to the outside world, is the inability to make signals of any kind in order to communicate with others. The counterpart to expressive asemia, receptive asemia, is the inability to understand such signs. This disease, which is caused by cerebral malfunctioning, serves as descriptive condition for a situation in which women have resigned themselves to their state of oppression. The consequences of this decision are rigidity and lifelessness.

In this piece, a bird is tied down on a platform with thin strings (the bird is already dead before the performance). The performer kneels in front of the bird and, using her mouth, pours hot liquid wax over the animal as well as over her own feet and hands: "the person and the bird as partners/parts in an anthropomorphic sculpture . . . demonstrate in the tension between the materials: bird (symbol of fantasy), wax (symbol of lifelessness) and human being, and in the tension between the forms (movement and rigidity) the tragedy of human self-representation."[18] With a knife in her mouth, the performer finally cuts through the wax and frees her hands. It is interesting in this connection that Export considered the knife to be a symbol of language, which by naming, separates the subject from the object.

The 16 mm short films *Remote . . . Remote . . .* and *Mann & Frau & Animal* (both 1973) can best be understood in tandem with the trilogy of sicknesses described above, since they depict the body as the field of psychosocial investigation. More personal than the performances, the films deal, respectively, with pain and pleasure. Both are, in a sense, performances for film. *Remote . . . Remote . . .* is shot against a backdrop of a large police archive photo of two children who were taken away from their parents because of abuse. Export is seated in front of this photo with a bowl of milk on her lap. After the initial identification

Asemia.

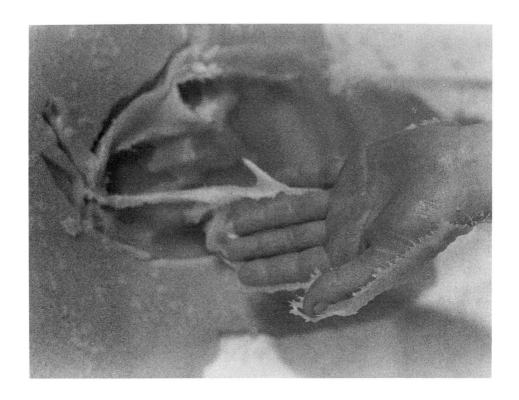

Asemia.

between the children and the performer, which is established as the camera cuts from the pupil of the child's eye to the pupil of the performer's eye, the action itself begins. With an Exacto knife, the performer first cuts the cuticles around her fingernails, but soon it becomes clear that this is not a cosmetic but rather a destructive activity, as the knife burrows deeper and deeper into the skin surrounding the fingernail. Blood begins to flow profusely and is periodically washed off in the bowl of milk held between her knees. In its visceral plasticity, this performance most clearly illustrates an aspect of much of Export's body work, namely, the externalization of internal states, a transfer of a deep psychology onto deep tissue, as it were. The same preoccupation with rendering the unconscious visible characterizes *Mann & Frau & Animal,* only here it is a question of investigating woman's pleasure. Two of the most tabooed images, orgasmic and menstruating female genitals, are displayed, in close-ups and medium shots, as candidly and matter-of-factly as the production of pain in *Remote . . . Remote . . . .* If patriarchal power is indeed predicated on the register of the visible, these two films are serious incursions into the mythological preserve from Dionysus to Christ that had granted women only auxiliary roles in the orgiastic display of pleasure and pain.

Export does not always conduct her attempts to visualize the biological givens for women on quite such unmediated bodily levels. *Homometer I* (1973) and *Homometer II* (1976) take up the question of women's reproductive function through symbolic representation. Bread—the "staff of life," symbol of nourishment, survival, life, and reproduction, encumbered with reverberations from every mythological system mankind has constructed thus far—becomes the burdening weight tied around the woman's legs as she crawls out of the ocean onto dry land in *Homometer I.* In the 1976 sequel, a street action, the performer ties a round loaf of bread over her stomach, intensifying the connotation of bread as source of life through the allusion to pregnancy. She asks passers-by to cut themselves a slice off the loaf.[19]

Remote . . . Remote . . . , 1973.

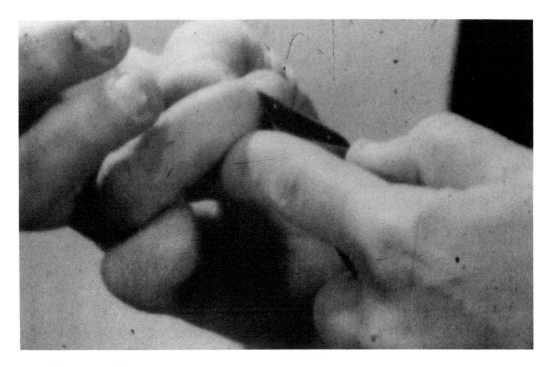

Remote . . . Remote . . . .

    With the trilogy of sickness, Valie Export reached a high point in body discourse that continued throughout the decade and probed deeper and deeper into the problematics posed so powerfully in 1973. In the same year Export also succeeded in joining her body work and its psychosocial context with the structural explorations of her media experiments. In the body interaction *I Am Beaten,* performed in 1973 at the Austrian Exhibition of the Edinburgh Festival, the performer lies flat on the floor with a mirror suspended directly above her. Next to her is a tape recorder with a loop on which the sentence "I am beaten" is uttered at regular intervals. The performer pronounces the same sentence, first by alternating with the tape and then gradually overlapping the tape until performer and machine are speaking the sentence in sync. The same performance was repeated a year later in Cologne as a video action that included two cameras, two monitors, and a complex relaying system from mirror image to monitors. On one level the piece deals with duplication, the duplication of woman through

Homometer I, 1973.

the machine as extension of the body, while also addressing image and sound duplication reproduction through art and technology and the reciprocal influence various levels of reality exert on each other. On another level, psychological structures, most obviously those of a masochistic and narcissistic nature, can also be traced. Export often chooses to combine technological facets with psychological disorders, claiming that there is a structural parallelism between the two (as, for example, in *Split Screen—Solipsismus*). Moreover, the performer s repetition of the sentence after the machine (an action with Big

Homometer II, 1976.

Brother connotations) alludes to social conditioning, if not to blatant indoctrination of the subject.

A piece that by its title refers back to this performance suggests a counterstrategy: *I [Beat (It)]*, performed five years later, in 1978. The bracketing in the title allows it to be read from left to right and from right to left and suggests a reversal of the earlier piece, *I Am Beaten*. It is a complex performance featuring, among other things, three monitors that show barking dogs. The monitors are arranged in a triangle, in the center of which, flat on the floor, is the life-size photograph of a woman. The

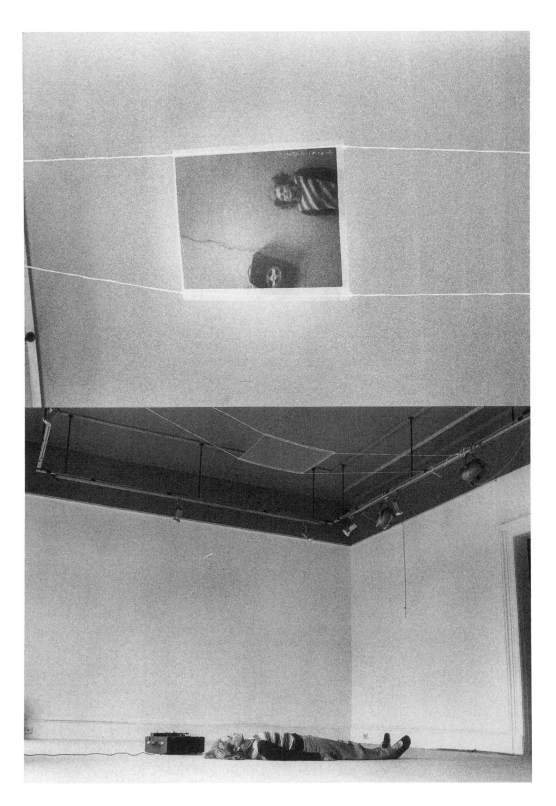

I Am Beaten, 1973.

I [Beat (It)], 1978.

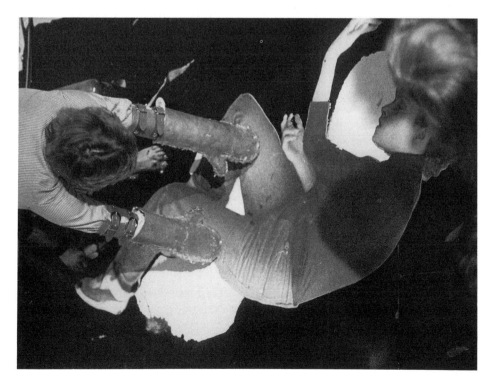

I [Beat (It)].

symbolism of the triangle refers to the chain of trinities, from the sacred father, son, and holy ghost to the profane father state, mother nature, and (male) ideology. The dogs, Pavlovian ones perhaps, persistently surround the woman with their "appellations." The performer moves in a spiral toward the photograph of the woman and spills oil from a container as she walks. Her movements are hampered by leaden bandages over her knees and elbows. As she lies down on the photographic image of the woman, a tape begins to drown out the insistent barking of the dogs, and the ambiguous word *"mehr/Meer"* takes over. *"Mehr"* means "more" of the same, but *"Meer"* means "ocean" and implies ritual cleansing, death and rebirth. The verbal ambiguity is also reinforced by a play on the French word *"mere,"* or "mother." It is the very ambivalence of this last word, the emphasis on the material signifier (the sound) rather than on the determinate referent, that reinforces the double-directionality of the title and at the same time refers to the earlier piece, *I Am Beaten*. The restaging of this earlier piece as *I [Beat (It)]* shows a change from passive voice to active choice, reminiscent of Freud's 1919 study of a fantasy called "A Child Is Being Beaten," which also features a shift in voice, but in reverse. In Freud's analysis, the active fantasy "the father is beating the child that I hate" is transformed into the passive "a child is being beaten." In terms of this fantasy, which according to Freud is a prevalent masturbatory fantasy among women, it is necessary to transform sadistic pleasure into masochistic pleasure. With this problematic in mind, one could think of Export's performance as asking why it is necessary for women to transform active into passive pleasure and redirecting this one-way determination to allow for reversibility and ambivalence.

In a critical essay on the Freudian notion of the unconscious, Jean-François Lyotard characterizes this notion as modelled on the mise-en-scène of Viennese opera. "We know that for Freud desire is what gives utterance to these primary [libidinal] messages, whereas the unconscious is their director and gives them a disguise in order to exhibit them on the stage. The accent is on deception."[20] The operations of the unconscious, some of which Freud described in *The Interpretation of Dreams,* are seen, according to Lyotard, as representing drives staged as symptoms. Lyotard challenges this model by pointing to the illogical nature of the drives, which Freud himself had acknowledged in his 1915 essay "Drives and Their Vicissitudes." Lyotard argues that since desire eludes interpretation, thanks to its "diachronisms, its polytopisms, and its paralogisms,"[21] it is not in need of disguises in order to be represented in the first place. He concludes that what is at stake for "post-modernism" is "not to exhibit truth within the closure of representation but to set up *perspectives* within the return of the *will,*"[22] and he subsequently describes will as "the will to create realities."[23] Export's performance *I* [*Beat* (*It*)] could be seen as an instance of just such a return of the will. In its acknowledgment not merely of ambivalence but also of polyvalence, it goes beyond the rehearsing of symptoms on the stage of the unconscious to open up new perspectives.

Export's interest in the unconscious as part of her self-exploration has never stayed in the realm of the private search for truth, but was from the very beginning aligned with an unorthodox rupture of the Freudian framework, in as far as it was directed toward the greater social question of women's predicament in patriarchal society. The artist's intent in this social investigation was not a mere rehearsal of the ills inflicted upon women, but, by making connections, incursions, and incisions in the social fabric, to create other possible realities. However, in all of this Export never neglects the importance of psychic pain and disfigurement sustained by individual women in the process of social codification, which warrants the concern with the unconscious and its symptoms: "The body is a territory for itself, for society . . . for the private sphere as well as the public sphere."[24]

Delta. Ein Stück (1977), first performed in Berlin at the centennial of the International Women Artists Exhibition (1877-1977),

Delta, 1977.

Delta.

Delta.

Delta.

is a powerful demonstration of how public and private are joined in the subjugation of women and how new perspectives are forged within that condition. The piece was repeated later that same year in Cologne. *Delta* bears the subtitle "persona performance," which is further described as "a drama in the continuum of distress caused by centuries of monogamy."[25] The performance is based on the observation of hand and shoulder symbolisms in representations that span a large historical spectrum and include the present time and its mass culture and mass media. A repressive ideological intent can be extrapolated from this archaeology of symbolic gestures. God the father, who places his hands in blessing on the shoulders of the married couple, and the priest, his representative, who ties the knot by slipping on the rings make sure "that the discourse between genders remains one in which men are in possession of mind, language and power and the role of woman is that of the body and is marked by loss of language and powerlessness."[26] The performance stage consisted of a triangular construct on which the words "Via Martialis" and

Wort

Antwort

Verantwortung

(word, answer, responsibility) had been written. Export describes the performance in the following way:

> Shoulder yoke—hand yoke:
> the juncture of the shoulder is replaced by the juncture of the hand
> With my wedged-in hand I write:
> the power of the powerless is silence.
> At the tip of the triangular plane there is the triangle that is again
> and again sounded by a plaster fist—to bring forth a sounding
> expression, to find its own sound.
> The scream—the language of pain.
> Axe and mouth form a cross, the tongue becomes a sharp metal
> edge, speechlessness turns into violence.
> The stigma of the body remains the stigma of the female sex, that
> mute energy whose will is sacrificed in the discourse of culture.
> The triangle becomes an axe. With the axe in hand the field of

action is shattered, because the power of women does not lie in the tedious projection of feminine renunciation on the way from Mary to the conjugal bride, we have found turnoffs from the via martialis that drive a definite wedge into the trade between body and mind.[27]

Video/Installations

Although the body is the most crucial point of engagement in Export's performances, technology and materials connoting technological usages such as electricity, gasoline, lead, etc., are always placed alongside the body. The value attached to technology is a potentially liberating one for Export. It follows her reasoning that the body of woman in patriarchy is biologically overdetermined, and in order to gain subjecthood women must abandon biology. The significance of including technology in the work with the body rests on these considerations: "Mixing heteronomous elements in the representation of the body points to the tendency to sacrifice the autonomy of the body in order to gain the autonomy of the [female] self. . . . "[28] While many of Export's performances use technological materials on the level of symbolic props, there is a group of body performances that are combined with video and in which video functions not just as a recording device but contributes in its own right to the overall effect. They are intermedia pieces in the sense Higgins proposed the term, designating conceptual fusion rather than a simple mixing.

Stille Sprache (Silent Language) is a ten-minute video performance that was begun around 1972 and developed over several years until it found its way into Export's first feature film, *Unsichtbare Gegner* (Invisible Adversaries, 1976). In *Silent Language*, the video process itself plays an important part in Export's reflection on the historical nature of female body posture. As the video demonstrates clearly, the possibility of instant replay in this medium allows for a "retracing" (*Nachstellung*) of the figures of women in historical paintings. The female figures' often quite peculiarly distorted body postures are copied by a performer in regular modern clothes and equipped with modern kitchen utensils. In the gradual process of superimposing

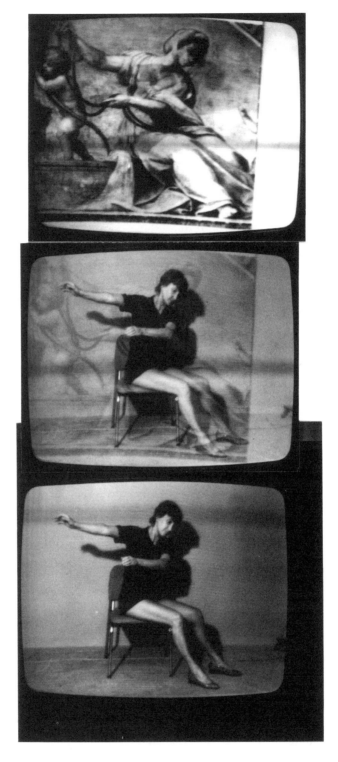

Silent Language, 1972–76.

VALIE EXPORT

the present performance onto the historical painting, the women's postures remain the same while all the other historical indicators of costume and custom have changed. For example, in the 1974 version of *Silent Language,* Export uses a female figure in a Renaissance painting by Rogier van der Weyden to provide a point of departure. The woman in the painting kneels and anxiously clutches the foot of the cross in a gesture of humble acceptance; the live performer emerges after the superimposition in the same posture but in the garb of a housewife clutching a broomstick.

The two-part video performance/body interaction *Movement Imaginations* (1974–75, performed in Linz, Austria), investigates an entirely different problematic. Not history but the phenomenon of inertia is under scrutiny for its potential to endure, and also to overcome, given hostile forces. Part one is a series of scenarios demonstrating the willpower necessary to resist extreme conditions with courage. These are concrete examples of the power of imagination, which butts against obstacles and limitations of all kinds. Export stands on the tips of her toes inside a small circle woven from barbed wire. The audience realizes that when she can no longer stand on her toes, she will pierce the soles of her feet. Next, she holds up a heavy weight with arms outstretched; gradually her arms sink down and out of the monitor frame. She presses a spring between her hands until they are folded in the position of prayer. She lies on the floor in push-up position, and remains like that until her head threatens to sink onto the pile of broken glass directly under her face. Finally, she sucks on a nail that has been beaten into a piece of wood until the nail comes out. Each situation creates tension between material laws and human willpower, contradictions that lead to a state of psychological splitting. The details of these actions are shown on video monitors in the foreground and in close-up, so that the audience can see the action from a distance as well as in cut-out fragments nearby.

The second part, *Movement Imagination No. 5,* tackles this rift and heals the split, thanks to the expanded capacity available to

Movement Imaginations, 1974–75.

VALIE EXPORT

Movement Imaginations.

the human body in the form of technology. The camera is directed so as to hold only the upper part of a room in its field of vision. A monitor standing in the lower part of the room shows the upper part on its screen and thus creates a split in the room. The performer, also standing on the ground, bridges the split by jumping into the camera's view, and thus appears on the monitor as well. The body bridges the divide. Export considered these imaginations of movement to be "bodily demonstrations of the passion of man to resist all extreme conditions as long as possible."[29]

Restringierter Code. Ein Stück (Restricted Code Performance, 1979), works like *Silent Language* with superimpositions, but the concern with the historical posture of women is broadened into a more species-specific questioning of the innateness of human expression. Departing from the preliminary distinction between "body language" (socially imposed gestures) and "body expression" (a reserve of unconventional,

Movement Imagination No. 5.

individual gesture), a new set of questions arises: What is the natural body and what is the cultural body? What is cultural and what is animal expression? Is there such a thing as "natural" body behavior? What is expressed in trance and ecstasy—what body? The performance, which involves an infant at the crawling stage, a dog, a hamster, and a bird, each in their respective cages (the child is in a crib), explores these questions. Dressed in an evening gown, Export is also inside a large wire cage. Food is put in the animals' cages as well as in the baby's crib. After receiving her meal, Export imitates the movements and eating habits of each of the other players. As her movements become more and more exaggerated, she finally picks one particular gesture to repeat and in this way induces a state of trance in herself. Two video cameras, one for Export and one for the animals and the baby, are continually recording the performance and rendering it on monitors in alternating superimpositions of Export and the others.

Export's exploration of the structural possibilities and communicative functions of technological media continued into the seventies with a major shift from 8 mm film to video as vehicle of investigation. The last short film, investigating the material conditions of the medium, was shot in 1971–72, not on 8 mm but on 16 mm stock. It is a three-minute meditation on time and space, and bears the descriptive title *Interrupted Line*. The camera is stationed in the back of a moving car and focuses on the dividing line ahead. At the same time, the frame includes the rearview mirror, in which the dividing line is continued behind the car. The car functions as the interruption in this time–space continuum, as "the seam of time, a bend between future and past."[30] Metaphorically, the car stands for the interruption of the everyday flow of time by the time of the film. With the exception of this film, all the other conceptual and structural studies of moving images in the seventies were done in video, whether video installation, video action, or just videotape. During that same period, Export also used conceptual photography to work out some of these analyses, especially those having to do with the construction

Restricted Code Performance, 1979.

Restricted Code Performance.

of images in serial sequences, with perspective, or with word-to-image transposition.

Autohypnose (Autohypnosis, 1969) and *Split Reality* (1967–69) were Export's earliest video installations. *Split Reality* was first shown in London and later in Graz, Austria (Steirischer Herbst, 1973), where *Autohypnosis* was also shown. These two installations pick up where 8 mm film left off. Expanded Cinema largely depended on strategies of separation and the partial replacement of its elements, and on attention to various levels of representation and their inherent differences—all of which aimed at an active or interactive relation with the audience. In *Autohypnosis* the participants are confronted with a diamond-shaped walking pattern containing code words such as "possession," "self," "development," "experience," "love," "renunciation," "knowledge," "discipline," "meditation," etc. The words are drawn onto a mat concealing sensors connecting the pattern to the video screen. Only by taking a prescribed pattern of steps can a participant activate the monitor. Curiously enough, these abstract concepts are called "codes," making clear the word-play medi-tat-ion (media action; German *tat* = "action"). The image and sound triggered by the correct code is a loop that shows a cheering crowd. This experiment exemplifies the reinforcement of social conformism. Because of the high degree of audience participation, *Autohypnosis* is considered a precursor to interactive video work of the late eighties and early nineties.[31] *Split Reality,* on the other hand, is mainly concerned with several levels of reproduction and separate codes—here quite simply sound and image—that go into producing a videotape. A record is played in front of the TV set. The sound has been turned off and the performer (Export) listens to the music of the record via headphones, singing along and thus reproducing the sound for the audience, which is perceptibly and visibly at one remove of its source.

Only one video action was actually a TV action dependent on television as institution in charge of transmitting programs for public viewing. *Facing a Family* (1971) is interested

Autohypnosis, 1969.

precisely in this aspect of program consumption as family enter-
tainment. Instead of showing a program, the piece confronts
the viewers with a typical reception situation: a family, as if
watching TV, looking back at them. Since the screen is the same
for both parties, a direct mirror effect—facing each other, facing oneself—is the result. The electronic and the real gaze cross
without interacting. The description of the action specifies that
the duration of this experiment is to be between five and twenty
minutes. The actual airing of the piece on Austrian television
lasted five minutes.

Two video installations, both of which took as their object the
processes of time specific to video, were also exhibited in Graz
(Steirischer Herbst, 1973). In contrast to film, the possibility of
simultaneously shooting and projecting footage, i.e., the possibility of "live" transmissions of events, annihilates distance and
eventually time itself. Likewise, video's ability to place a long

Split Reality, 1967–69.

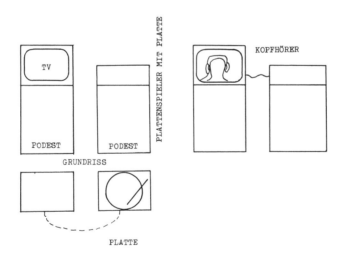

SPLIT REALITY
Video Poem, 1967/69

Vor dem Tv-Apparat wird eine Schallplatte gespielt. Der Ton ist abgedreht. Ich höre sie im
Tv-Apparat mit Kopfhörern mit, und singe die unhörbare Platte.

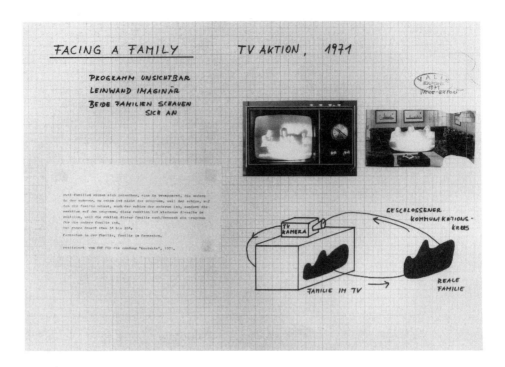

Facing a Family, 1971.

shot and a close-up of a detail side by side in the same image, or to mount events that are taking place in different locations onto the screen together, relativizes time and space, the dimensions of time—past, present and future—accessible to human manipulation to an unheard-of degree. Everything then becomes a question of distribution, which as Export insists, can be handled positively or negatively. The positive aspects are illustrated spatially in a glass box that served, one might say, as a utopian motto to accompany Export's pieces at this '73 exhibit. The box contains two mutually exclusive elements—air and water—in separate compartments, with one serving as aquarium for fish, the other as cage for a rat, demonstrating the beneficent distribution of pertinent information by the media. The two installations *Zeit und Gegenzeit* (Time and Countertime) and *Interrupted Movement* are based on fairly simple concepts. In the first, the process of melting ice is recorded on tape and then

Time and Countertime, 1973.

played backward, while an actual plate of ice cubes is placed in front of the monitor showing the process of ice melting in real time. *Interrupted Movement* is similar in its arrangement to the 16 mm short *Interrupted Line*. In this case, two cameras are mounted back to back in the middle of a street, one recording the oncoming traffic, the other the backs of cars driving away. These video recordings are continuously telecast to two monitors inside the exhibition space. The two monitors face each other in such a way that they leave enough space for the viewers to walk between them. The continuous movement in the street is thus interrupted by the gallery space, and the visitors can safely cross the flow of cars. This experiment was repeated in more complex terms in *Zeitspalten–Raumlücken* (Time Fissures–Space Gaps, 1975).

The 1974 videotape *Schnitte* (Cuts) is a city project that explores the notion of inner and outer, private and public spaces in a combination of sound–image counterpoint and serial

Monitor I, Interrupted Movement, 1973.   *Monitor II, Interrupted Movement, 1973.*

montage. The piece is conceived in two parts, the first of which establishes the inside/outside dynamic by combining a 45-second shot from an apartment window into the street below with the sound of incidental noises inside the room. This inside/outside shot is followed by the reversal of the camera position, a 45-second shot through a window into an apartment coupled with the sound of street noises. The second section of the tape is a serial sound montage accompanied by a visual parade of windows: the camera begins and ends with the image of the whole façade of the building and then proceeds to focus on the outside of each window at five-second intervals. Each window has its own characteristic noise, suggesting what is going on inside the rooms behind the window panes. In this way, each of the windows functions like a loudspeaker, broadcasting the private sphere into the public. A similar sound–space exploration is the subject of a twenty-minute videotape entitled *Raumsehen und Raumhören* (Seeing Space and Hearing Space, 1974). The tape works with extreme reductions and minimal use of materials to arrive at an elementary demonstration of sound and body movements in space. It begins with a single note produced by a synthesizer. The tone is repeated periodically and moves both from side to side in the room as well as forward (toward the camera) and backward. Each spatial position is characterized by a change in the quality of the tone, either with respect to volume, repetition interval, or the sound coloration (*Klangfarbe*). At the same time,

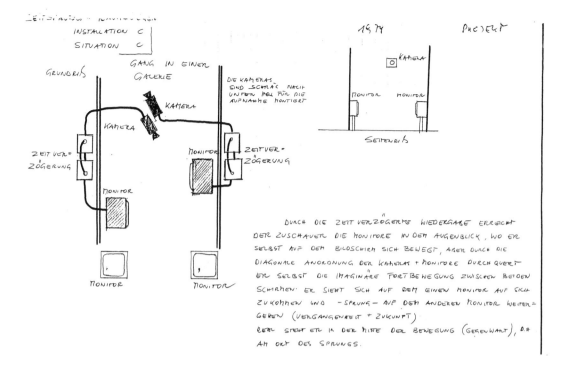

ZEITFISSUREN - RAUMLÜCKEN

INSTALLATION C
SITUATION C

GRUNDRISS

GANG IN EINER
GALERIE

DIE KAMERAS
SIND SCHRÄG NACH
UNTEN HGL FÜR DIE
AUFNAHME MONTIERT

KAMERA

KAMERA

ZEIT VER=
ZÖGERUNG

MONITOR

ZEITVER=
ZÖGERUNG

MONITOR

MONITOR

MONITOR

1974   PROJEKT

KAMERA

MONITOR   MONITOR

SEITENRISS

DURCH DIE ZEITVERZÖGERTE WIEDERGABE ERREICHT
DER ZUSCHAUER DIE MONITORE IN DEM AUGENBLICK, WO ER
SELBST AUF DEM BILDSCHIRM SICH BEWEGT, ABER DURCH DIE
DIAGONALE ANORDNUNG DER KAMERAS + MONITORE DURCHQUERT
ER SELBST DIE IMAGINÄRE FORTBEWEGUNG ZWISCHEN BEIDEN
SCHIRMEN: ER SIEHT SICH AUF DEM EINEN MONITOR AUF SICH
ZUKOMMEN UND -SPRUNG- AUF DEM ANDEREN MONITOR WEITER=
GEHEN (VERGANGENHEIT + ZUKUNFT)
REAL STEHT ER IN DER MITTE DER BEWEGUNG (GEGENWART), D.H.
AM ORT DES SPRUNGS.

SITUATION D
INSTALLATION D

ZEITSPRUNG - RAUMLÜCKEN   1974   PROJEKT

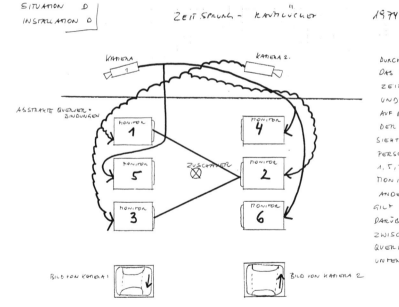

KAMERA 1   KAMERA 2.

ABSTRAKTE QUERVER=
BINDUNGEN

MONITOR 1
MONITOR 4
MONITOR 5
ZUSCHAUER ⊗
MONITOR 2
MONITOR 3
MONITOR 6

BILD VON KAMERA 1   BILD VON KAMERA 2

DURCH ZWEI VERTEILER ERSCHEINT
DAS BILD VON KAMERA 1 GLEICH-
ZEITIG AUF DEN MONITOREN 4,5,6
UND DAS BILD VON KAMERA 2
AUF DEN MONITOREN 1,2,3
DER ZUSCHAUER IN DER MITTE
SIEHT ALSO DIE BEWEGUNG DER
PERSON/AUTO AUF DEN MONITOREN
1,5,3 GEBROCHEN, DA AUF
MONITOR 5 DAS OBJEKT EINE
ANDERE RICHTUNG HAT. DASSELBE
GILT AUCH FÜR DIE GEGENSEITE.
DARÜBER HINAUS GIBT ES NOCH
ZWISCHEN DEN BEIDEN SEITEN
QUERVERBINDUNGEN (FORTSETZUNGEN +
UNTERBRECHUNGEN DER BEWEGUNG)

DAS BILD WIRD IMMER ZEITVERZÖGERND ÜBERTRAGEN
SODAß AM MONITOR 3 +6 DIE BILDER VON KAMERA 1
+ VON KAMERA 2 GLEICHZEITIG ZU SEHEN SIND
1 BEWEGUNG WIRD ZERSPLITTERT ZU EINER MULT.-DIREKTIONALEN (U.U.
AUCH ANTI-DIREKTIONALER) BEWEGUNG

Time Fissures–Space Gaps, 1974.

the recording of the tape was conceived of as a performance with spectators who could watch on monitors how the four cameras and a split-screen device are capable of complex time, space, sound, and movement structuration. Export described the experiment with this equation: music + sculpture = melody. A kind of meditative melody develops indeed in the sequence of six different compositions. The spectators present at the performance also can observe that the performer, the sole point of visual reference in the otherwise undecorated room, remains standing on the same spot, while the four cameras and the split-screen device create the illusion of movement as the body appears on the monitors to the left or right, in front or back, or split in various combinations as the sounds' visual counterpart. In the last part of the tape, different body parts and different sizes are mounted together on the split-screen.

Another equally interesting structural exploration of the possibilities of the new medium is the video performance *Adjungierte Dislokationen II* (Adjoined Dislocations II, 1974–78), in reference to the 8 mm and 16 mm expanded movie of the same title made by Export in 1973. The video project was conceived in 1974 but was not executed until 1978, when it was shown at the *pro musica nova* festival in Bremen, Germany. As in the expanded movie, this video project explored problems of spatial perception and experience. It also featured a frontal and dorsal camera strapped to the performer's body. However, instead of the rambling explorations of the movie, an artistic space was created in order to clarify concepts. The artistic environment represented the three possible coordinates of space: horizontal, vertical, and diagonal, each orientation depicted by lines painted on a wall. The fourth wall was left open to include the audience within this structure and as part of it. This particular aspect is possible only with video because of its capacity to record and transmit simultaneously. The performer, fitted with cameras in front and back, paces a staked-out three-dimensional spiral course (which also exists in the form of a sculpture placed to the side of the scene) in the middle of this

 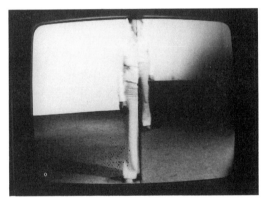

 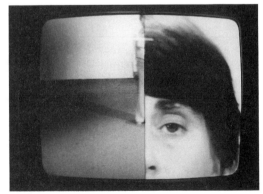

Seeing Space and Hearing Space, 1975.

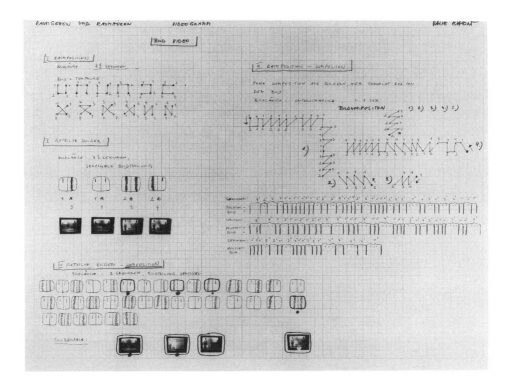

Seeing Space and Hearing Space.

space, while the two cameras record images appearing on eight monitors (four on each side of the environment), the frontal camera corresponding with two monitors mounted on the top rows, the dorsal camera with those on the bottom rows. Aside from the beautiful optical patterns arising in close-up detail as a result of the body/camera movement, the audience can also observe the entire environment at once: "The body of the environment and the environment of the body melt into a total picture."[32] The point of this performance was not to demonstrate the different uses of video by pointing to its documentary or technical capacity, but to employ video in finding solutions to aesthetic problems or in asking new questions of art. In this case the created artistic environment—the three walls with horizontal, vertical, and diagonal lines and the spiral walk in the middle—are classical spacial arrangements that are transferred, through the movement of the cameras, to the monitors to create new representations and new images. These images in turn become part of the environment as a whole.[33]

One aspect of *Adjungierte Dislokationen II,* not specifically emphasized in this performance is the reduction of three dimensional space to the flat surface of the monitor screen. In the 1975 video sculpture *Inversion,* this aspect becomes the main point of investigation. A black ball mounted on a rotating stick describes a circle in its course of movement. One quarter of the circling movement is transferred onto a monitor and appears to be a straight line. This segment is copied in turn by three other monitors in a time lag until the circumference of the whole circle is covered, but in form of a straight line. This experiment in geometry attempts not to square but to straighten a circle, and the final image is a horizontally moving point forming a line (the line consisting of points).

The opposite and also far more complex operation is the video installation *Split Video Mobile.* It converts a straight line into a circle, but in an interactive situation that necessitates an audience for its completion. *Split Video Mobile* also dates back to 1975 and actually was conceived before *Inversion.* In this

Adjoined Dislocations II, 1974–78.

Adjoined Dislocations II.

Inversion, 1975.

installation, six cameras are mounted on a wall in the shape of a semicircle. The participant enters on one side of the semicircle and walks in a straight line to the other end. The six cameras, each with its own visual corridor, cover the entire line from beginning to end, also partly overlapping each other's segments. At the end of the line the participant returns to the entrance by walking along the back of the semicircle wall. There, six monitors are mounted in the same position where the cameras are placed in front. Through a slight delay in transmission the participant is able to watch her own entry and progression along the straight line, which comes to an end just as she arrives at the entrance. In this way the circle—this time not in a strict geometric sense but in the sense of a circuit—is closed. While *Inversion* dealt with the reduction from three to two dimensions,

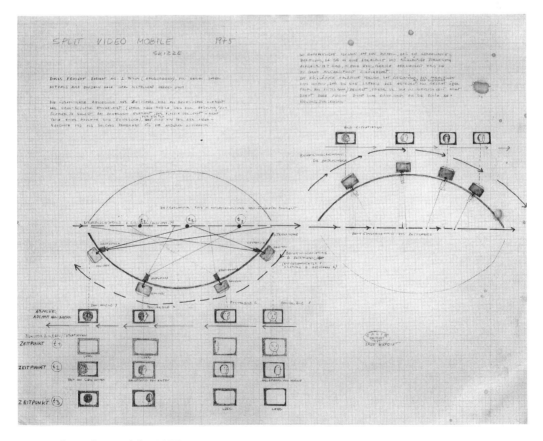

Split Video Mobile, 1975.

Split Video Mobile analyzes the perception of space and time through the interaction of human and technological capacities.

This possibility of reciprocal human and technological perception was the focus of an earlier interactive video installation, *Trans-Object* (1973–74). In this case the emphasis was on the perceptive mechanism of the technological object. A translucent (glass) water container, holding the same amount of water in cubic centimeters as there were inhabitants in the respective cities of exhibition, released one cubic centimeter of water for each visitor. This subtraction was then transferred to another container whose water volume showed the sum total of people who had seen the exhibit up to this point in time. Visitors' perceptions on the installation's meaning can, of course, vary. One possible response would be to establish the ratio of experimental art lovers for that particular city.

It should be evident at this point that video continued in the seventies where Expanded Cinema had left off. For Export, the versatility of video made it particularly suited to her continuing investigations into the precondition of the medium itself. Most frequently, Export deployed the categories of space and time as parameters of this inquiry. But other questions were raised as well: the relation between image and sound, the effect of two- versus three-dimensionality, and also sociological categories such as public and private space. As was the case with Expanded Cinema, the role of the audience in these exercises is rarely out of view. At the very least, the video/installations demonstrate to an attentive audience what the possibilities of the medium are; ideally, the spectators will actually be able to participate and interact with the pieces.

3

Photography

Moholy-Nagy predicted in the twenties that photography would displace traditional painting because it was a medium more suited to the technological age.[1] In less radical terms, Walter Benjamin assessed the impact of technology on traditional forms of art as liberation from its aura of quasi-religious radiance based on the notion of authenticity and originality. But in the time that has elapsed since these early avant-garde speculations about technology—which had as much to do with the possibilities of industrial mass production of commodities and wealth as they did with photography and film—the predictions have worn thin. History and the canon, archives and curators have entered the field and counteract the potentially leveling effect (which to Benjamin and Brecht connoted democratization) of technology in photography and film. As Susan Sontag has pointed out, photography's "exhibition in museums and galleries has revealed that photographs do possess a kind of authenticity,"[2] and that an aura accumulates around technologically reproducible artifacts simply with age or from the unavailability of the kinds of materials used during a certain epoch. In the meantime, the tables have turned completely, and now the icons

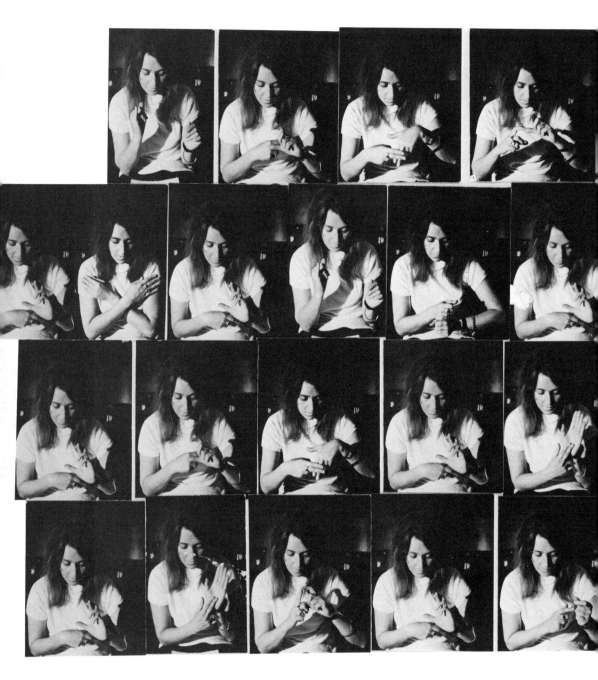

Finger Poem, 1968.

VALIE EXPORT

of the technologically reproducible world have attained fetish status in Pop Art.

At the same time, photography's other determinant, its identification with documentary and "objective" realism, which, to be sure, has never been anything else but "conformity with . . . the social definition of the objective view of our world,"[3] was problematized. Scruples were advanced, in particular by avant-garde movements such as Conceptual Art, which were skeptical of visual representation to begin with. Yet to the extent that "the real referent" continues to be "felt to be dominant in photography,"[4] all manner of confrontation with the representational dimension of this medium would seem to be fundamental to its exploration as an art form. In yet another turn of the avant-garde's debate, concern has shifted from divesting the work of art of its fetishistic religious aura to preventing realist representations from claiming object status and thus succumbing to fetishization once again.

Since the late 1960s and early 1970s, Valie Export has adopted photography as one of her fields of aesthetic exploration, often in conjunction with or preceding her performances and installations. And, as she does with each new medium, she immediately staked out its formal and material possibilities. This experimental interest is most purely expressed in her conceptual serial photography. Like the structural films of the sixties and seventies, these photo experiments investigate the material base, as well as the dimensions of space and time, that contribute to the photographic process. Here, as in most of the procedures that were considered "conceptual" at the time, "photography becomes a means for representing concepts thought out in advance. The goal is a representation on as many levels as possible, which opens up a field of associations for the subjectivity of the viewer."[5] Export's first serial conceptual photographic exploration, *Fingergedicht* (Finger Poem, 1968), had also been a performance demonstrating the body as medium of communication and information which was subsequently recorded on video. In the photographic series, each letter of the alphabet is represented in a separate photo showing Export reproducing the letter with her hands. *Finger Poem* bears the subtitle "Ich zeige die Zeige mit den Zeichen im Zeigen der Sage," which is the artist's extended (and quite untranslatable) version of Heidegger's concern with the ontology of the image, arrived at by way of her bridging of gestural, written, and spoken language. (It should be noted that *Finger Poem* and all the following instances of Export's photographic explorations discussed here are only representative examples of a much larger body of work.)

"Foto–Raum" (Photo–Space, 1971) parallels some of the attempts made in the expanded movies to let the eye of the camera retrieve what is normally hidden from the human eye. Spatial extension beyond the walls of the gallery room is achieved by mounting enlarged photos on each wall, the ceiling, and the floor of the view behind it. Another parallel to the expanded movies'

Photo–Space, 1971.

Leap of Space, 1971.

France, 1973.

aspect of interactivity, as well as to the concerns of structural films of the seventies, can be traced in a five-piece sequence entitled *tektonisch rezeproke bewegung* (*Tectonic Reciprocal Movement*, 1971). The aerial photograph of a city is enlarged in successively greater increments, such that smaller and smaller details of the view are blown up to fit the original photo size to the point that the photographic texture begins to lose its recognizable outlines and look like a close-up of an abstract pattern. The five pictures are mounted on a gallery wall and it is up to the viewer to adjust his/her distance from each photo to allow for clear perception. Thus the time and space dimension is introduced through the movement of the viewer, through his/her point of view in relation to the photos.

Spatial exploration is also the aim of the three-part *Raumsprung* (Leap of Space, 1971). A façade of balconies is photographed not from the opposite side of the street (i.e., the horizontal, frontal axis) but vertically from above, working its way from the top balcony downward to a view of the pavement. By dispensing in this way with classical representational forms and a preconceived notion of what balconies should look like, a whole new visual pattern emerges that attracts and engages visual curiosity and interest rather than short-circuiting it through familiar images. Although primarily a spatial exploration, time is also captured in the serial aspect of the sequence, which represents movement in this case not from the point of view of the viewer but rather of the photographer. In another three-part photo entitled *Frankreich* (France, 1973), the vertical perspectival axis of *Leap of Space* has been converted into a sweeping semicircle from the view of the photographer's feet on the pavement of the street to the frontal/horizontal shot of a house across the street, ending in a view of clouds in the sky crisscrossed by wires and antennae fixed to roof tops. This tripartite photo is further complicated by the fact that each part consists of three separate shots, in each case taken from the same position but visibly set off from each other by a jarring seam. The introduction of the category of time through serial juxtaposition foregrounds the idea of movement and thus of camera placement—in the first case of the entire camera position down a vertical axis and in the second case a tilting upward of an otherwise stationary camera. As is the case in all of the conceptual procedures, the unity and continuity of space and time is dissolved and processes are represented in their partiality and segmentation. In this way photographs become "sites of imagination which allow a variety of views and representations to permeate each other."[6]

The suggestion of movement implicit in serial photography is heightened in *Landschaftsraum–Zeitraum* (Landscape Space–Time Space, 1972), in which the car in motion acts as the camera. The windshield is marked with a white line. A picture is taken once every minute through the windshield. The white line is the time line; it becomes the signifier of the time continuum. The photos represent the spatial dimension as well as the segmented element of interruption, as opposed to the continuum of time. This exercise perfectly encapsulates another ambition of Export's conceptual photography: visual experiments that break down the barrier between the categories of space and time, spatializing time and giving space a temporal dimension.

Landscape Space–Time Space, 1972.

Leap of Space was published in 1973 in a small volume entitled *stadt: visuelle strukturen* (city: visual structures), which accommodated much of Export's serial conceptual photography of the previous year, with the exception of *zeitgedicht* (time poem, 1970), a 24-piece series (one photograph for each hour of the day) of the same shot of a street photographed from a high angle and from identical camera positions. Recording the objective passage of time and its attendant changes in light as well as in the amount of traffic in the street is a suitable prelude to a number of pieces shaped by subjective time or thematic criteria in the remainder of the volume.

Time Poem is followed by *linie* (line, 1972), which consists of twenty-three photos of cityscapes taken at regular intervals along a straight line drawn across the map of Vienna. This cross-section of the city, extending from its outskirts to its center (St. Stephan's cathedral) and back to the suburbs, calls attention to the variety and composition of the city's neighborhoods. It corresponds to the stated intention of the authors (Export and Herman Hendrich) of *city: visual structures* to induce in Viennese readers an interest in the structures of their immediate environment and to stimulate new ways of thinking about it. This exercise of traversing the city along a line drawn straight through the map is repeated on a smaller scale in *gemeindebau* (community center, 1972). Here the line passes through the building in twenty-four successive pictures, each taken of the wall opposite the photographer's entry to the room. This

Time Poem, 1972.

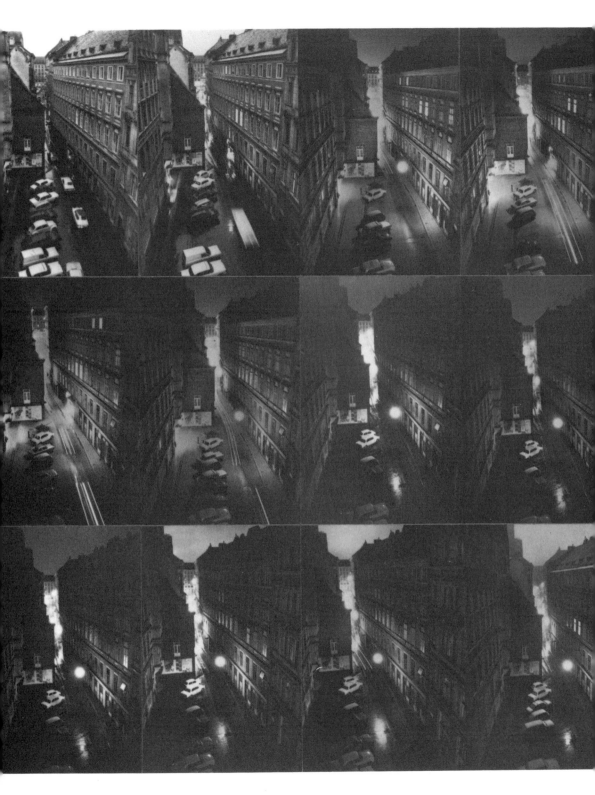

photographic passage finishes with the view of the street. Two other serials in *city* are thematically chosen and adequately described by their titles: "23 kinderspielplätze" (23 playgrounds for children, 1972), and "wahringerstrasse no. 204–no. 1" (Wahringer Street no. 204–no. 1, 1972) an eight-piece sequence of entrances to houses taken at seven-minute intervals.

The last part of this volume is a pun of sorts. Entitled "halte–stelle," it plays with a range of meanings, from "bus stop," to "stopping place," to "holding this place." The latter meaning also provides the structural principle for the seven-piece sequence of images. The camera literally holds the bus stop in its view, not in order to mark the passage of time (as in the introductory piece), but to foreground it as a place in a variety of spatial constellations, with and without a bus, with and without pedestrians, and with some variation in distances. This playful excursion into semantics appears again in other pieces not included in this volume: *Schriftzug* (1972), meaning "hand writing," literally translates "writing train" and makes its punning point in a three-part sequence of photographs of an actual train, first in a close-up of the word "Schriftzug" written on one of its cars, then repeating the same shot from a medium distance, and finally showing the train as it vanishes into the distance. Trains and their marvelous suitedness to perspectival studies became the object of *Zug I* (Train I, 1972). *Train I* is a visibly set-off montage of a train curving in its center part with vanishing points to the left and to the right. The train was photographed from many different points of view, which were combined in the final montage into one image, no longer providing a realistic representation of the train but instead an assemblage of different spatial and time segments. Similarly, the 1972 *Leiter* (Ladder) is a montage of a ladder, again with a central camera focus that makes the top and bottom parts of the ladder recede to some extent, giving it an unusual O-shape.

Export's photo-literature experiments do not always require a pun. In *Schatten* (Shadow, 1971) and *Ebbe und Flut* (Ebb and Flow, 1974), the relation between word and image is all that seems to be at stake. In the former, the shadow of two hands is

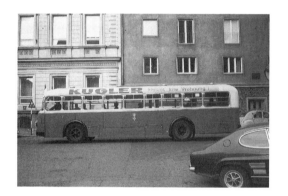

"halte–stelle," 1972.

Train I, 1972.

cast over the word. In the latter, the words are written on the sand just in front of the receding waves. The ephemeral quality of the object (the shadow) in the first case, and of the word in the second, establishes a balance of importance or insignificance between the lexical and the iconographic sign. This balance is also extended to the indexical signs in a 1973 photo called *Be"weg"ung–Spur* (Movement–Trace), with another pun, this time on the middle syllable *weg*, meaning "gone," which points to the erasability of what it shows: footprints in the sand. These sign function studies belong to an anagrammatic repertoire that turns up again and again in Export's work in other contexts and combinations. In this respect, *Syntagma* comes to mind as a veritable store-house of anagrammatic exercises.

In 1972 Export began work on what is perhaps the most significant series of her early photographic experiments, '*Körperkonfigurationen in der Architektur* (Body Configurations in Architecture, 1972–82). These images combine the female body and structural geometric concepts inspired by architectural forms. Accordingly, they explore the body as ornament and its

accommodation with its environment, as well as a "visible externalization of internal states"[7] in the body's arrangements themselves. "Insertion," "adaption," "addition," and "elevation" are some of the principles which shape the body's adjustments to its architectural environs. Here the anagrammatical structure of Export's work is evident in some detail. She transposes these simple structural and architectonic principles onto the body, letting the body act as their complement. Yet upon closer scrutiny these cultural and geometric forms also prove to have their origin in the body, establishing in this way a reciprocity of formal transpositions. And further, when placed in a narrative field, as in *Invisible Adversaries*, the aspect of externalized internal states is foregrounded as it releases the female subject's point of view to permeate geometric form with emotional content. Another whole cycle of *Body Configurations in Architecture* was shot in 1976 specifically for this film. Suzanne Widl, the film's protagonist, is the photographic object giving expression to her state of estrangement and alienation from her environment. An ornament at best, she demonstrates the qualities of "adaptation" and

Ladder, 1972.

Ebb and Flow, 1974.

Body Configurations in Architecture, 1972.

Body Configurations in Architecture, 1976.

Body Configurations in Architecture, 1982.

"insertion," merging with the architectural forms in an anxious attempt to escape from a hostile environment. And in a further anagrammatical development, *Syntagma*, an ostensibly non-narrative, experimental film concerned primarily with formal and structural investigations, is able to draw narrative import from the cumulative power of transpositions attached to a brief sequence of *Body Configurations in Architecture*.

Another kind of anagrammatic sequencing is based on semantic rather than formal-structural considerations. For example, in different contexts, the meaning of "bed" becomes a highly complex field ranging from *Coercion*, the title of a 1972 photograph picturing a woman sleeping while wearing ice skates, to a place of regeneration, as it is at the end of *Invisible Adversaries*. Export explains these transpositions in terms of what might be called emotional-psychic experimentation: "In 1972, when I was particularly preoccupied with the representation of mental states, I wanted to go to bed with lead cuffs around my wrists and ankles and to sleep one night with them on. When I tried it, I was overcome by terrible fear, a feeling of loneliness, of helplessly exposing myself to sleep in this constrained position. When I tried to sleep one night with skates on, I had the oddest sequence of dreams and next morning when I woke up I experienced a feeling of relief. At that time I made a whole series of such experiments, e.g. going to bed in mountaineering outfit, in man's clothes, roller skates, with paper masks, paper clothes."[8] This whole ambiguous field of meaning is carried over every time the signifier for "bed" appears, as it does frequently in all of Export's work: the "Stiegenbett" (staircase bed, 1972) as part of *Body Configurations*, bed sequences in *Syntagma, Menschenfrauen*, and *Invisible Adversaries*, or the installation *Geburtenbett* (Birth Bed, 1980) to mention only a few examples. In this way, Export succeeded in combining her overriding concern with the body with emphasis on thought, language, and the artist's vision and imagination all of which are introduced through "Conceptual Art." While she participated in the general trend that developed from "the activation of the body as an artistic

"Context Variations," 1971.

medium at the end of the 'fifties and beginning of the 'sixties" into "the activation of the brain, the apparatus of thinking, the power of imagination,"[9] she did not abandon the body in her explorations at the end of the '60s, and thus was able to stave off the intellectualization of art that marked much of this period. In a characteristic attitude of bridging rather than dividing mind/body, subject/object, and external/internal states, Export concentrates on their reciprocal interaction instead of their oppositionality:

> The parallel between landscape and the mind, and between architecture and the mind, is mediated by the body because, on the one hand, the parallel has its origin in the external opposition between mind and body, and also because the body bears the stamp of other factors, just as the landscape does. The landscape shows the marks made by space and time, that is, to be more precise, the disposition of its parts, such as trees, rocks and hills, shows such effects. This disposition of parts of the body makes up bodily poses; they also show the stamp of inner states and express them. This analogy between scenic and bodily arrangements, these common forms of revealing mood, have served since the beginning of pictorial art as projection surfaces for expression: external configurations, whether they are in the landscape or in the picture (which thus turns into the landscape) serve as the expression of internal states.[10]

A larger study of semantic, contextual changes is compiled in *Zyklus zur Zivilisation—zur mythologie der zivilisatorischen prozesse*" (Cycle of Civilization—Toward a Mythology of the Processes of Civilization, 1972). In the first part of this cycle, five photos taken from previous actions, performances, and expanded movies (*body sign action*, *Eros/ion*, and *Cutting*)—all of them dealing with the body as bearer of cultural signs and as material surface of cultural inscription—are juxtaposed with an anthropological photograph of

VALIE EXPORT

"Context Variations."

a tribal tattooing ceremony. The reference to the body as cultural artefact avoids the pitfalls of the binary opposition of nature and culture in its emphasis on the process of alteration itself. The human activity of inscribing, writing, creating a new surface becomes a third term which favors neither nature nor culture but instead lowers the threshold between them by pointing to the dependence on materiality coupled with the pleasure and the necessity of transformation. The second part of this cycle, sub-titled "Kontext Variationen" (Context Variations), brings all of these elements to expression. It is a sequence of five photos taken of an Action performed in Vienna in 1971 involving a loosely piled-up stone wall, a rather rudimentary artefact in a natural setting. Subsequently, the wall is set afire in what might be described as either cultural or natural interaction since it makes use of a natural force. The third image shows the wall after it has been burned as it is being transported to an urban environment. The grassy plot left deserted after the wall has been removed con-stitutes the fourth picture, and in the last photo the stone wall can be seen rebuilt in one of the busy streets in the center of the city. During the actual action of exhibiting the stone wall in an urban context, the five photos were also on display. Like fire, stones bridge natural and cultural forces. Stone is *the* primor-dially natural material and paleontological record of the earth's geological history, yet, at the same time, and in these shifting contexts, it breaks down the borders between nature and culture, emphasizing its constructedness in a natural environment and its naturalness in the midst of urban structures. Export prefers such triangular fields of meaning rather than binary oppositions, since they facilitate a more complex transformative approach.

Contrasting contexts are also the main point of experiment in a triptych entitled *Haus des Meeres* (House of the Ocean, 1975). The three separate photos comment on each other in their diversity, displaying vistas of the ocean, a path in the forest, and a telegraph pole, respectively. Further, each picture has its own source of disparity within its parameters. Thus, the house at the edge of the ocean is not just an architectural contrast to the

House of the Ocean II, 1975.

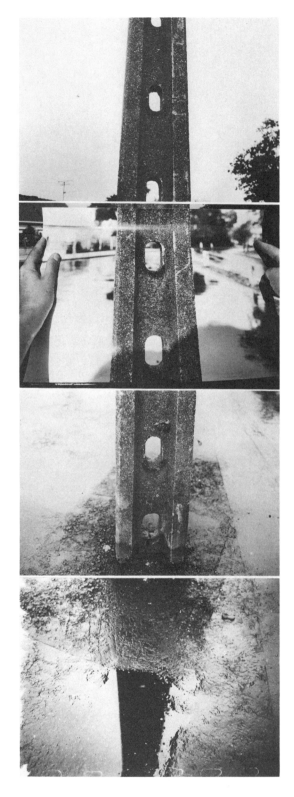

House of the Ocean III, 1975.

natural landscape; it is a military installation, and thus is devoid of all picturesque connotation. The second and third photos are structurally disrupted in as far as their middle sections are layered, i.e., fitted into the original photo to complete the picture. To augment this break and emphasize the two generations of photos, the hand fitting in the section is photographed along with it. Export calls this procedure "photographic mise-en-scène" (*inszenierte Fotographie*). Several other series of photographs taken around 1973–74[11] continue to conceptualize the human body in this field between culture and nature. These are in some ways the counterpart to *Body Configurations in Architecture* in that they explore natural landscapes in conjunction both with the body and with geometric figures. *Aus dem humanoiden Skizzenbuch der Natur* (From the Humanoid Sketchbook of Nature, 1973) is a conjunction of photography and drawing. Different views of the dune landscapes in Belgium are supplemented morphologically with drawings of various parts of the body, such as an arm, a hand, or a mouth. *Kon-figurationsstudie* (Configuration Study, 1973) and *Aus dem geometrischen Skizzenbuch der Natur, I, II, III* (From the Geometric Sketchbook of Nature, I, II, III, 1974) are similar explorations with the slight difference that the photographer's hand is in the foreground, completing, underlining, or contrasting the natural contours of the dunes. At the same time, this foreground/background setup lends itself to perspectival comparisons. Morphological studies of one natural constellation with another—for example, the outline of a mountain range against the sky compared to the outline of a beach against the ocean—were also part of this particular photographic concern. By far the more frequent comparisons, however, involve the human body. *Körperfigurationen in der Natur* (Body Figurations in Nature, 1972–74) looks at the entire body in its various accommodations with its natural environment. Again, basic geometric rules and considerations are invoked to describe and at times subsume both the shapes of the body and of nature to their rigor.

From the Humanoid Sketchbook of Nature, 1973.

From the Humanoid Sketchbook of Nature, 1974.

Body Figurations in Nature, 1972–1974.

Body Figurations in Nature.

These geometric compositions involving the body both in its natural as well as its urban architectural surroundings represent a systematic attempt on Export's part to thematize the double structure of the human body, a concern that has remained central to her work. Taking Leonardo da Vinci's *Corpus More Geometrico* as emblem of her deliberations on the human body, she interprets this famous drawing to stand for a common measure and proportion between geometry, the body, and the mind. The photographic depictions of body postures in these "configuration" sequences, which employ geometric designs as an aspect of the body's expressivity, are based on these insights. The double structure of the body as both material and mind, as instrument and sign is further emphasized by the drawing's superimposition of the circle and the square, signifying both movement and stasis. In its double structure the body also becomes a cultural record: "I use the photographic fixing within a physical context (house, city, country) not because movement should articulate the significance of the body, but because I want to force the body's code out of the frozen history of culture, which is a history of silence."[12]

Similar considerations presided over *Nonpareille* (1976), a three-part photographic study of female body postures in Botticelli's *The Spring*, as well as *Petri/fikation* (1976), a retracing of poses of two women in William Blake's *Naomi Entreating Ruth and Orpha to Return to the Land of Moab*. These studies of female posture in historical paintings reappear in another medial transposition, the videotape "Silent Language" from *Invisible Adversaries*. They also gave rise to a whole series of photographs (as well as drawings) of madonnas modelled after Michelangelo's *Pietà* in body posture but fitted with various insignia of housewifely chores, such as a knitting machine in *Die Strickmadonna* (Knitting Madonna, 1976) or a washing machine in *Die Geburtenmadonna* (Birth Madonna, 1976).

These photographic explorations of the body (which frequently is the photographer's own) show it as doubly determined by material nature and cultural signification. This assertion is

Petri/fikation, 1976.

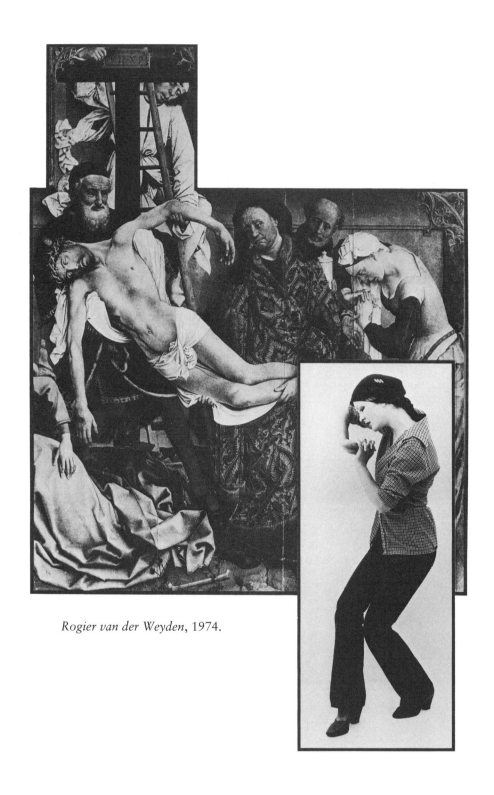

Rogier van der Weyden, 1974.

carried onto another level even more broadly transgressive of neat categorical distinctions. In a series of photos entitled *Ontologischer Sprung* (Ontological Leap, 1974), Export departs from Heidegger's notion that the ontology of the image is static being. She confronts nature and the natural object with the process of representation, placing specific emphasis on the conditions of photographic technology. In this process, a three-piece sequence of layered photographic representation, Heidegger's

Knitting Madonna, 1976.

Madonna with Vacuum Cleaner, 1976.

axiom proves untenable. Ontology is challenged by the copy, which as "the double is the simulacrum, the second, the representative of the original. It comes after the first, and in this following, it can only exist as figure, or image. . . . Through duplication, it opens the original to the effect of difference, of deferral, of one-thing-after-another, or within another: of multiples burgeoning within the same."[13] Technological reproduction strips the images of the notion of "being" through its ability to shift their object determination in multiple ways. By layering different levels of reproduction, an image-within-the-image effect is created that foregrounds considerations of constructedness rather than "being," displacing the focus from the image object to the viewing subject. The layering also differentiates the codes, and through constant transposition they ultimately become free-floating. The photos thus are readable on one level as differentiated codes. Thus, the ontological status of the "reality" of objects in the pictures is challenged by pointing to various techniques that connote greater or lesser degrees of closeness to nature. Thus, the first black-and-white image of feet in the sand looks more like a reproduction than the second layer of the same objects, feet and sand—which appear this time in color. The warm flesh tones of the feet standing on the black and white photo make it seem more "real" than the original shot. Finally, on the third layer, an oriental rug (cultural artefact par excellence) is placed as background to the previous two layers, and the photographer's own feet are placed on top of the feet in black and white, covering them over in this way. The contextual shift from natural material (sand) to cultural artefact (rug) as well as the photographer/subject stepping onto what appears to be the most entrenched object layer, provide enough border crossings, conceptual breaks, and points of comparison to come to the conclusion that the "ontological leap" is a leap out of ontology via technology.

In Export's most recent digital photography, the aspect of technological manipulation looms large. In some ways this technique allows for the same effects that virtual reality creates: a greater distance from any given material reality coupled with a greater semblance of reality. A photograph is not just an iconic representation but is related to the real through a causal, indexical trace given in the photochemical process. The digital image, however, is intrinsically free from any such direct ties to the referent. This contradiction between distance to and semblance of reality built into the technology itself calls for vigorous frag-

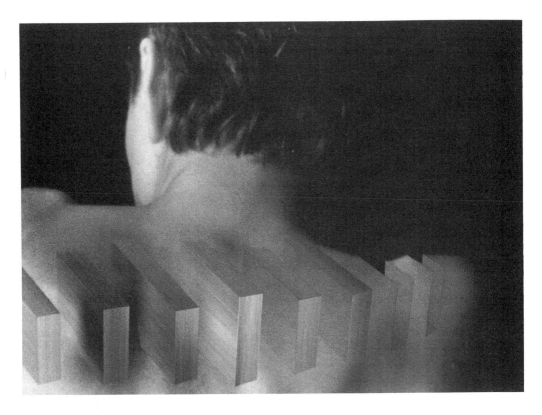

Twi-Topon, 1991.

mentation in representation in order to counter the illusion of
reality. In a sense the difference is akin to that between theater
and film, wherein film, because of its total lack of intrusion of
the presence of actors, props, etc., is more removed from the real
and at the same time able to create a more convincing effect of
reality. Likewise, in digital photography, where the trace is no
longer a direct one, but everything is simulated, the power of
the imaginary is that much greater. The comparison is, of course,
only a partial one, since the difference between theater and film
revolves around the presence or absence of the real, whereas
photography and digital technology take the whole problem one
step further in the direction of absence, with or without a trace.

Export's continued exploration of bodies in architecture,
urban landscapes, or simply in relation to pieces of furniture is
presented with an unprecedented degree and possibility of

Self-Portrait with Staircase and Skyscraper, 1987.

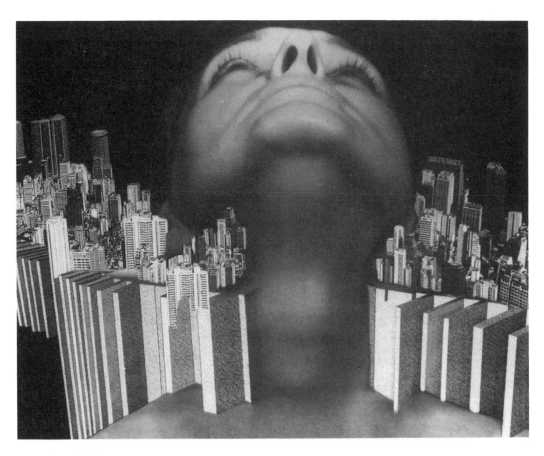

City, 1989.

textural blending that her *Body Configurations* had aimed at but had not been able to achieve to this degree of technical perfection. The procedure of textural mapping made possible by various computer programs is a kind of photomontage without the cutting and pasting. Instead, it allows the texture of the photograph to be extended into new shapes, as in *Twi-Topon* (1991), in which the neck and shoulders are flawlessly turned into an abstract architectural landscape. Superimposition of buildings upon bodies or faces, causing multiple distortions as in *Selbstporträt mit Stiege und Hochhaus* (Self-Portrait with Staircase and Sky-scraper, 1987), are among the most exciting techniques since they thoroughly counteract the illusionistic potential of the new medium, allowing Export to add new dimensions to her thematic of the body in culture.

In *Stadt* (City, 1989), the sphinxlike face of a woman takes center stage in the skyline of a modern metropolis. Her neck and bent-back face both tower over and support the cityscape. The combination of distortion and seamless fit (the houses seem to be growing out of her shoulders, as in *Twi-Topon*) is a long way removed from *Body Configurations in Architecture*, which dealt with bodies bending themselves out of shape around architectural features without the benefit of montage. Here the situation is somewhat reversed: the houses are huddling around the strong neck and face of the woman. In his comments on Atget's Paris photos, Walter Benjamin sees the city in these pictures to be "cleared out like an apartment which has not yet found a new tenant." Benjamin concludes that this was in preparation to a "salutary alienation between humans and their environment"[14] fully expressed in Surrealist photography. What was "salutary" about this alienation for Benjamin—the clearing away of familiar relations in favor of details unlocking their secrets to the politically trained eye—has also been a crucial ingredient in Export's continued investigation of women's place in culture. For Export, the city has always been the privileged site for testing unfamiliar relations. In this most recent work, the woman's face in *City* or in *Self-Portrait* announces, through all the distortion, a mirage, so perfect an illusion of unreality that it could be a vision of the new tenant, becoming bolder with each new technological invention.

4

Invisible Adversaries

Manneristic gestures and signs of a deviating and crumbling identity, when a person is trying to escape from the coercive structures and injurious forms of communication. Female body language refusing to react according to pattern when recognizing the message: leaden fear weighs down the skin forcing it to slide off the glass walls of a phone booth.

Deep lesion when the difference between observer and observed disintegrates. When the image in the mirror displays a mask it has already discarded. To watch oneself like someone unknown with a profound longing for ultimate identification.

When sentences are said that are devoid of general meaning, when you turn off all the lights and open the dark abyss behind you, never to come back, when the lost self is crying, unable to part, when children become enemies, it is no longer a question of testing a theory of existence, but to save individuation, to save bare life in a reality of frenzied destruction (even at the price of se/cession).

A communication that is the bearer of hatred is opposed by a behavior of vulnerability. When dreams and sleep, when the storage basin of subconscious thought become the site of battle signalling the tearing-up of all existing pictures, we shall see the real picture through the rent, the drama of human self-realization.

On the search for home the noose slid round the neck.

—Valie Export

By the mid-seventies Valie Export had established herself as one of Europe's foremost feminist performance and installation artists. Her work in avant-garde film had already earned her the recognition of and invitation to participate in all the major European avant-garde film festivals. Now Export posed herself the task of integrating film and all of her different experimental projects in video, performance, and installation art. The result of this effort was Export's first feature film, *Unsichtbare Gegner* (Invisible Adversaries, 1976), a 100-minute, 16 mm color film. Peter Weibel, Export's former companion, collaborated on the script, which became the vehicle for accommodating in vignette fashion a great number of already finished pieces. Like Lévi-Strauss's bricoleur, who "addresses himself to a collection of oddments left over from human endeavors,"[1] Export conceives of the interpolation of ready-mades into the script in terms of signs. As self-contained signifying units, they comment like the chorus in Greek tragedy on the action of the plot.

As soon as traditional categories such as action and plot are mentioned, the need to qualify these terms arises. While it is true that the script has narrative elements that can be outlined and events that can be recounted, it is by no means a plot with an exposition at the beginning, complications in the middle, and resolutions at the end. Instead, the events in the life of the young woman photographer, Anna (Susanne Widl), loosely cover the period of a year, during which she observes a progressive dejection in her own spirit that drives her to look for increasingly morose subject matter for her camera. Her explanation for this state of decay is surprising, to say the least: she thinks she is affected by what she sees as an invasion of a foreign enemy power, the Hyksos. The Hyksos were an ancient Egyptian tribe renowned for their sudden appearance and equally sudden disappearance. Export, who had been fascinated with this people ever since her youth, finally gave them a place in her film.

In this classic scenario of a case of paranoid schizophrenia, Anna perceives the invasion as a doubling effect in people. Similar to the dramatic scenario of the Hollywood film *The Invasion of the Body Snatchers* (with which Export was not familiar at the time of shooting), in which people's bodies remain the same externally but are internally occupied by the invading power that alters their behavior completely, the increase in aggressive behavior all around her convinces Anna that the hostile Hyksos have indeed taken over this planet. Her daily encounters and her meticulous photographic record-keeping of her impressions lack development. Instead there is a repetition of crises or a crescendo of anxiety in nearly every episode of Anna's quotidian experience. Whatever development does occur is on the level of Anna's progressive awareness of what is ailing her, rather than that of plot and action.

It is tempting to conceptualize the script stylistically in terms of realism and in opposition to the abstract-symbolic quality of the inserted video, photo, or installation pieces. Such a clear-cut distinction, however, is hard to uphold upon closer scrutiny. Certainly, there are more realist elements in the script than in the inserts, but the boundary is by no means impermeable. The most banal everyday conversations, the most casual gestures can suddenly freeze in the flow of the narrative and become stylized to such a degree that they resemble the inserts. The reason for this mixing of styles, or rather this lack of restraining boundaries between different levels of representation, can be found in the process of film production as a whole. The script was initially fairly rudimentary, not much more than a sequence of scenes and dialogue. Sometimes the dialogue developed spontaneously, especially in the passages that deal with Anna and her lover, Peter. Export supplied the lines for Anna's part, whereas Weibel not only wrote but also acted the character of Peter. Although autobiographical, these passages are not realistic reproductions of actual conversations; rather, they are a distillation of the states of feelings from a number of relationships experienced by each author over the years. Other dialogue passages, on the other hand, were carefully written and planned.

The visual execution of the script was not calculated in advance or described in writing, but in most cases came about spontaneously during the process of shooting. Chance was allowed a large margin in shaping the film, and this principle was not just applied to the construction of sequences but to the inclusion of materials as well. The sequence in which the young woman poet is videotaped and then interviewed, for example, found its way into the film because Export had seen her performance right around the time she was shooting the film and had been impressed by the poet's naive self-representation. The final conception, organization, and composition of *Invisible Adversaries,* however, happened at the cutting table. It took Export eight weeks to edit the film, during which time she recomposed many passages, including those provided by the script. The fine-tuning of matching or contrasting sequences follows principles of association and commentary available to the artist. Export's love of the classical avant-garde, Cubism, Surrealism, and Dadaism can be gauged by the meticulous attention to the collage effect evident in the overall fabric of the film.

The invasion fantasy of *Invisible Adversaries* is at the same time the story of a splitting, the classic Freudian case of a split personality—namely, the case of Schreber, who also experienced his double nature as a kind of occupation by another force, in his case a divine one. Anna is in a sense a reversal of the classical example. Whereas Schreber aspires to the position of abject female vis-à-vis his commanding Lord, Anna, already placed in the position of female and quite abjectly so, aspires to achieve command and control over her life through her camera eye. While the film makes no effort to discount or reject Freudian theories of the unconscious and of its concomitant split psyche (acquired in the process of a defence against castration), it playfully displaces the ingredients of this theory to point to the fact of historical difference. More than anything, it takes seriously Freud's own caveat regarding feminine sexuality by pointing to the power of its socially determined condition. This disruption, played out against the background of a tradition, is already provided by the setting: Vienna, birthplace of psychoanalysis, approximately a century after that momentous event.

The film begins with a montage of short sequences which point to the connection between the split in Anna's psyche and her interaction with her environment. These sequences are structured so that they alternate between inside and outside spaces, private and public spheres. A zoom-in on a newspaper whose headlines coincide with the title of the film alternates with a shot of the interior of Anna's room, where she lies asleep in her bed. The camera then moves back out through the window, and in a long circular pan surveys the rooftops of Vienna. Radio news without visible source announces that the goal of the strange invaders, the Hyksos, is the destruction of Earth through an increase in aggression. These warnings about the Hyksos, their likeness to humans, and their contagiousness, are mixed in with ordinary news about Austrian party politics and international affairs. The camera returns to the interior of Anna's apartment, as her phone rings and she goes to answer it. When she realizes that nobody is speaking at the other end, she becomes extremely agitated. At the end of these alternating sequences comes the first recognition for Anna, via her own mirror image, that she has a doppelgänger. The reflection in the mirror does not perform the same movements as Anna: it applies lipstick while Anna just watches.

What is remarkable about the sequences that thematize public and private realms is that they simultaneously break down the

Anna and her doppelgänger

dividing lines between those realms in yet another attempt by Export to bridge traditionally accepted oppositions, a practice which has been theorized as "border-crossing."[2] Similarly, subjective perceptions are not rigorously marked as such. On the contrary, the film delights in making objective Anna's subjective fears of an invasion, when it takes them up as fact in the public organs of newspaper and radio. Likewise, the cinematic point of view is complicit with her from the beginning when it portrays the cause of her anxiety, the "other" Anna in the mirror reflection, as an objective, visually comprehensible menace.

This opening sequence of alternating public and private spaces is followed by a similar alternation between shots of Anna's work place and professional activities and shots that give some insight into her relationship with Peter. Again, the borders are blurred; each territory is informed by the other. The subjects of her photographic work are continuations of her experience and sexual encounters with Peter, and conversely her intimate time with him is shot through with conversations from recent trends in intellectual and art history. Thus, in a scene in the bathroom, Anna's attempt to dry herself after her bath is not only diverted into Peter's sexual games but also leads into a string of quotations from Lévi-Strauss's *The Raw and the Cooked*. Most interesting in this sequence, however, is the occasion to review Export's own photographic and performance work of the time. Some of these works are ascribed to Anna in an unproblematic identification of the filmmaker with the actress, while others take Anna herself as acting subject.

The first set of photographs is directly related to Anna, as she is seen developing them in her darkroom. They are images of female genitals in close-up, very much in the confrontational mode of much of Export's performance work, militantly revealing that which is forever hidden because of its implied threat to phallocratic imagery. The sound track delivers its own tragicomic commentary to this sequence. Every time the photos are dipped into the developing solution, a male voice makes hoarse retching sounds. The effect of this is at first comical, in that the voice seems to emanate directly from the pictures; the second take is tragic, since it reminds us of the all too familiar deprecation of the female sex that the photos set out to confront in the first place.

The ensuing sequence of images is among Export's most important photographic work in the seventies. Long before Cindy Sherman's impersonations were recognized as the "deconstruction of the supposed innocence of the images of women projected by the media"[3] and filed away under the rubric "postmodern," Export had finished a series of collages of various madonnas and pietàs with the same deconstructing intent. In each case the Christ child or body of Christ was replaced by different household utensils, such as a vacuum cleaner, a washing machine, and other symbols of women's drudgery (see chapter 3). These collages are related to the video piece entitled *Silent Language*, which also appears later in the film. Here, the woman's body becomes the material sign—a kind of time machine—in an investigation of the past as she deduces her "position" in society from the "position," the social gestures, of other women through history.

The last performance insert in this alternating sequence is the traumatic dream scene of Anna walking in ice skates down staircases and through city streets, escalators, lawns, etc., projected above her prone, sleeping figure in bed. At times the film within the film takes over, and the bed drops from view, or else Anna's figure in bed becomes part of a photomontage of several staggered layers, not only of beds but also of differing layers of photographic materials, some in color and some in black and white. The skate-walk ends by cutting the blades of one of the skates across someone's (presumably Anna's) thighs and circling the blood traces onto an ice surface. This performance is based on a series of experiments Export performed in 1972, which involved her attempt to sleep with skates on, in a mountaineer-

Skate-walk dream sequence

VALIE EXPORT

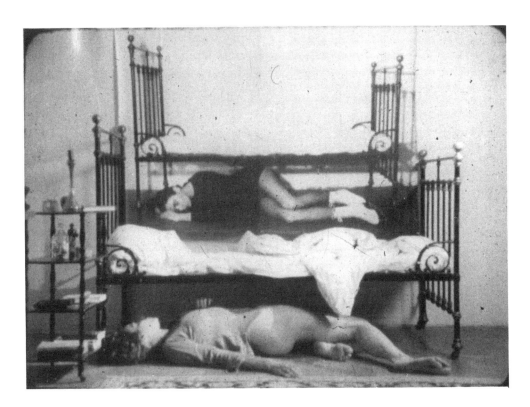

Anna in bed, dreaming

ing outfit, or with her joints locked in lead cuffs (see Chapter 2).
As in the first alternating sequence, this passage also closes with
Anna's doppelgänger image in the mirror. This time the mirror
reflection is crying while Anna is turning away. Finally, an
anonymous hand appears on screen and writes the words
"Silence is the power of the powerless."

This exposition of Anna's circumstances and psychic condition is amplified in the subsequent sections of the film that focus
on Anna's environment. This segment might be entitled "The
Hyksos," for it illustrates the external conditions that surround
Anna daily and are the model for her fantasies of the invasion
of an evil force. The discrepancy between Anna's rather exotic
invader fantasy, accompanied by quotes from George Mathieu,[4]
and the banality of evil in Vienna's quotidian exchange is quite
humorous, but as is the case with all the humor in *Invisible
Adversaries*, it has a sinister undertone that at times escalates to

a crescendo of horrifying proportions. In this sequence, for example, the aggression she encounters from a shopkeeper and a meterman is carried over into her conversation with Peter, which ends in a fight and is subsequently amplified in a veritable symphony of fighting scenes—of couples in cars, in public places, in phone conversations, and so forth—until the sheer dynamics of repetition propels these scenes onto another plane of intensity, namely the documentary footage of full-fledged warfare. Once again we see the filmmaker's inclination to cross over from what appear to be separate categories, both formal and discursive, and to make connections between personal and political as well as everyday and extraordinary (and even catastrophic) incidents. This tendency ultimately aims at mending the rift within the self so painfully experienced in the mirror image; Export describes it as "profound longing for ultimate identification." At the same time, one might object that the "deviating and crumbling identity" Export attributes to the attempt "to escape from the coercive structures and injurious forms of communication" is little more than the narcissistic refusal to accept the necessity of lack and desire as the precondition for entering the symbolic, to speak in recent psychoanalytic terms. Or, to use instead the feminist version of those terms, are we witnessing someone who is "excluded by the nature of things?"[5] Peter's question during the fighting scene—"What do women want?"—echoes Freud's inquiry of half a century ago, and, followed by Peter's caustic conclusion that "women are parasites," testifies to the continuing puzzlement over the "dark continent" of patriarchal society, as well as pointing to the virulent underside of psychoanalytic discourse.

The next sequence dramatizes the effect of the escalation of violence in the outside world on Anna's constitution. This episode consists of three exquisitely balanced but totally silent pieces that in and of themselves could be separate performances, but work together in the narrative to afford an insight into Anna's state of mind. In their silence they work at the furthest psychic recess of consciousness, as it were, which explains their dream quality. The first of these images shows Anna running through a gateway into an arenalike plaza with a fountain in its center. The place is totally deserted except for what looks like a row of people sitting on the rim of the fountain. As Anna comes closer she realizes that the people are only two-dimensional cardboard replicas, and at that point there is a brief insert of a murmuring crowd on the sound track. She frantically circles around the fountain only to collapse and turn into a cutout photographic figure herself. This depiction of a subject in crisis literally revolves around the metaphor of the fountain. Traditionally associated with the wellspring of one's innermost being, the fountain is ingeniously linked to the outside world, in as far as it is surrounded by people. Inside and outside are interrelated, and it is the recognition of the unreality of one of the terms that causes the collapse of the whole.

After this almost archetypal description of a "crumbling identity," the other two segments address more specific aspects of Anna's life that are equally affected by this general breakdown. One concerns the traditional site of women's work, the kitchen, where the customary routine is turned topsy-turvy. In a fascinating montage, the film switches back and forth between the cutting of live animals and fruit or vegetables. As a visual pun on filmic cutting, it makes use of typical moments of suspense as the knife comes down on the head of a bird or a turtle, but finishes the cut on a piece of fruit or bread, chopping that into two pieces instead. Similar sensations of anxiety are aroused when the content of the refrigerator turns out to be a baby.

The other area of Anna's life, her photographic work, is also adversely affected by this crisis. Her selection of a demolition site as photographic subject is not the only indication to that effect. The series of cross-cuttings between the actual site and the lab where the photos are being developed ends in her burning a picture of a natural landscape, as if Anna wanted to parallel the demise of nature with the demolition of the houses. Through this act, Anna acknowledges that the time when she was interested in beautiful landscapes is past, and elsewhere in the film she often

People at the fountain: cardboard replicas

Cut-out replica of Anna

Signs of Anna's breakdown: the baby in the refrigerator

complains to Peter that her subject matter is becoming more and more depressing.

At one point when Anna is looking for his support, Peter offers an explanation of what ails her. In response to a verbal pun on Anna's part, which is only awkwardly rendered in English,[6] Peter tells her: "A nice pun, but it shows what kinds of mechanisms you have succumbed to. You take everything too literally. In your case the word has certainly become flesh too soon." This annulling of the difference between the sign and its referent is also thematized in the metamorphosis of Anna herself into one of the two-dimensional cutouts. Anna is well aware of her equivocation and takes it into account in her investigations, even as she wonders about the nature of her perception: "My visual work is like a monologue . . . I cannot believe the reality of my environment . . . my paranoia surrounds me."

In her analysis of the woman spectator, Mary Ann Doane points out that "there is a certain naivete assigned to women in relation to the systems of signification—a tendency to deny the process of representation, to collapse the opposition between the sign (the image) and the real."[7] As if to remind herself constantly of this crucial difference, Anna assiduously records every facet of her environment, sensing a certain kind of protection in these ramparts of frozen images. They also represent the search for an "objective" corroboration of her subjective perceptions. Anna's difficulty in determining subject and object may also be related to the alleged inability of women to separate sign and referent. In any case, the clarification of these terms might be described as Anna's specific quest.

More than anything, the protection Anna's photography affords her is a visual, structural one, an attempt to hide behind the camera and to reverse the axis of looking in order to escape from the passive position of being the object of the look, which feminist film theory since Laura Mulvey has analyzed as the place of women in traditional cinema. The active look of the camera, commonly assigned to the male, is the position Anna claims for herself. For the supposed ease with which women spectators identify with filmic representations also has to do with their own status as image, which assigns to them the register of space. "The male is the mover of narrative while the female's association with space or matter deprives her of subjectivity."[8] From the position behind the camera, on the contrary, it is possible for Anna to address the question of whether the frightening changes she observes in her environment are actually occurring independently of her own psychic condition. Such a degree of sovereign consideration would not be available to her if she remained identified with the silent image, receptacle of other identities. There is an opposing movement, then, to the

Ontological Leap, 1974.

Ontological Leap.

Ontological Leap, 1974.

Facing page, from top to bottom:
Ontological Leap I, II and III, 1974.

Journey to a Non-Identified Symbol, 1973.

Blood Heat, 1973.

Birth Bed, 1980.

Split-Monument, 1982.

Birth Madonna, 1976.

Invisible Adversaries, 1976.

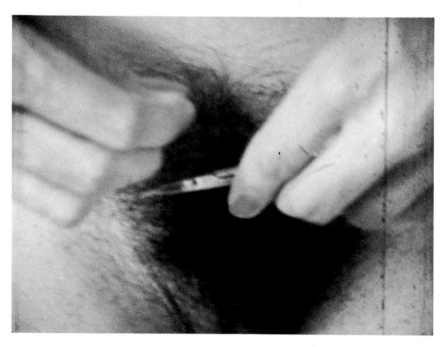

Invisible Adversaries.

The Practice of Love, 1984.

The Practice of Love.

The Practice of Love.

The Practice of Love.

The Practice of Love.

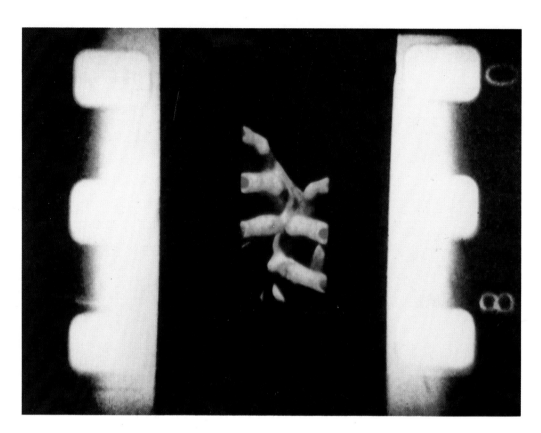

Syntagma, 1983.

Syntagma.

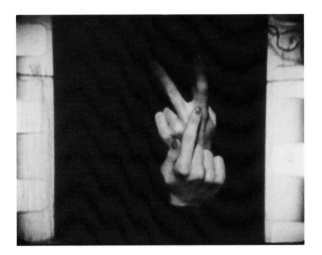

Syntagma.

Syntagma.

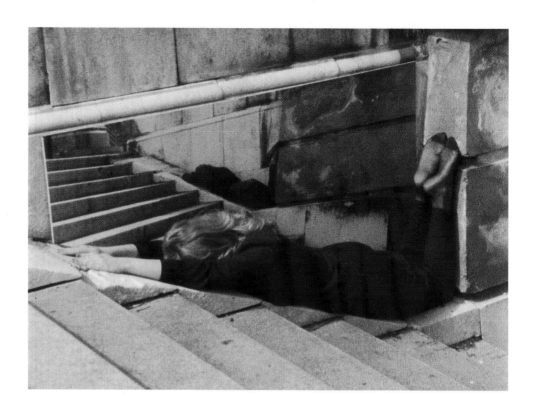

Syntagma.

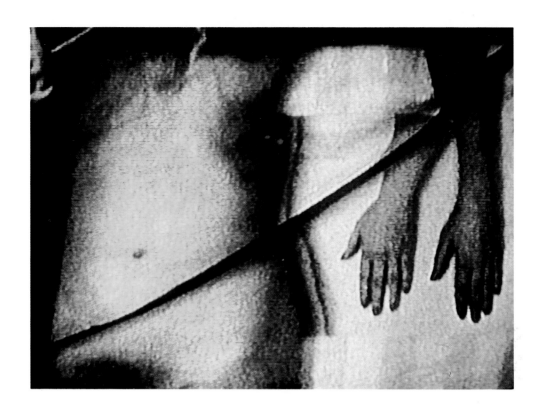

Syntagma.

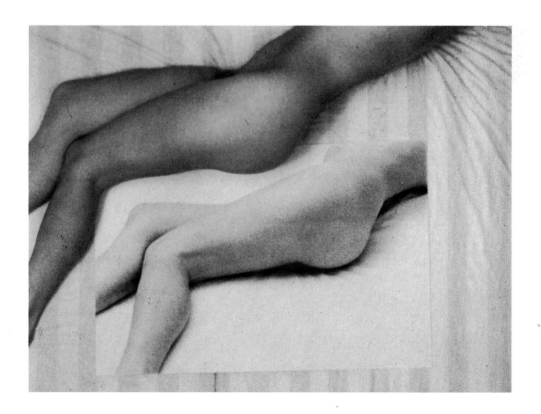

A Perfect Pair, 1986.

A Perfect Pair.

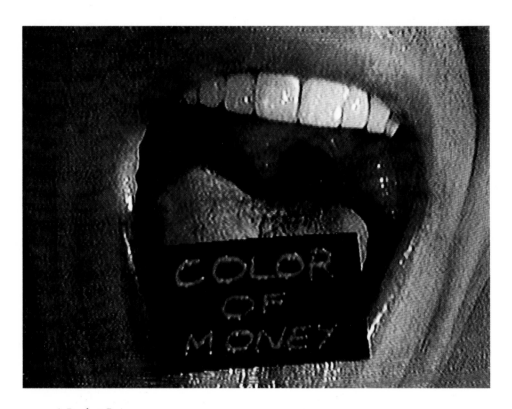

A Perfect Pair.

Invagination, 1988.

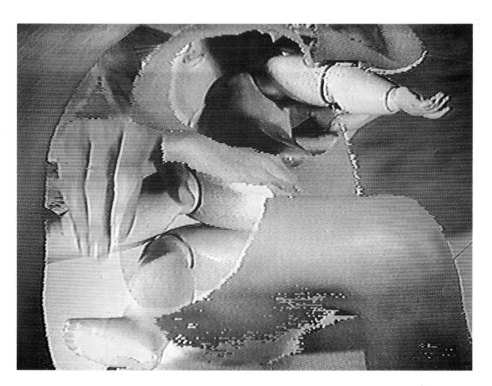

Voices from an Inner Space, 1988.

Zerstörte Löwener Bibliothek, Sarajevo, 1914, 1991.

destruction and conflagration Anna is busy recording. What is breaking apart is her identification with a world in which her subjectivity is relegated to the margins, and what is slowly and painfully surfacing is her insistence on understanding and working through the mechanisms of her marginalization.

A fine demonstration of the process of marginalization is the photographic performance work entitled *Body Configurations in Architecture,* subtitled "Visible externalization of internal states, the body arranging itself with its environment." This work occupied Export between 1972 and 1976 and is included in the film to great advantage. These spatial-geometric explorations are juxtaposed after a brief cameo appearance by Helke Sander, during which she responds to Anna's inquiry "What makes the human being a woman?" by referring to Friedrich Engels' historical explanation of the plight of women as a consequence of the natural division of labor in early patriarchal societies. As Anna curves herself around street curbs, fitting her body into niches and corners of buildings, it becomes clear how little space is allotted to her. Despite her assignment to the spatial register, her body's arrangements within its environment look very much like vanishing acts. Woman's body, Export contends, is literally "selfless," not her own: "She is allowed to function through her body only in relation to man, in relation to society."[9]

Despite his critical protestations, Anna's lover Peter is still a representative of the world she is contending with. During their intermittent encounters, it becomes increasingly apparent that Peter completely misses the point about Anna's condition and prefers to take refuge in fashionable theories, informing her condescendingly that human beings are "side effects of various overlapping systems" and that love is no more than a "tug in the prick." Nevertheless, the character of Peter is by no means stereotypical. On the contrary, he is given a large range of expression, from annoying macho male, to spirited lover, to tender and conciliatory companion. If that were not the case, Anna's grief at breaking up with him could not carry the dramatic

Peter and Anna

weight it does; her sobbing collapse in the bathroom of a train succeeds in touching rather than embarrassing the viewer. Their final encounter, already distanced through the interplay of monitors which act as two ghostly counterparts to their conversation, draws up the tally: While Peter hates the idea of love and friendship and is committed to self-sufficiency, Anna defends these values and acknowledges her need for love. It is little consolation to her that Peter describes her as an "angel," whereas he feels his own life to be a kind of hell in which he wants to be alone.

Peter's self-description fairly justifies Anna's Hyksos anxiety, as do the many incidences of violence she observes. What is striking is that only she seems to suffer in their relationship, as if she were carrying his share of emotional investment as well as her own. Precisely this notion of woman's vicarious emotional burdening is a predicament Tania Modleski observed in her study of Hitchcock's films: "the male finds it necessary to repress certain 'feminine' aspects of himself, and to project these exclusively onto the woman, who does the suffering for both of them."[10] And Kaja Silverman (upon whose essay "Masochism and Subjectivity" Modleski bases her observations) developed the notion of projection in her book *The Acoustic Mirror* to launch a major challenge to the psychoanalytic explanation of the construction of female subjectivity. Silverman concurs with Lacan in acknowledging that symbolic castration precedes the recognition of anatomical difference, but she takes this acknowledgment a step further when she attempts to articulate "the relationship between castration—symbolic castration—and the traumatic discovery anatomized by Freud."[11] Cinema, she contends, has the potential to reactivate the trauma of symbolic castration in the spectator and at the same time works well to allay the fears thus aroused. Putting sexual difference in place is one possible safety net for the male viewer. The mechanism of

projection, akin to processes in film viewing, allows for the transfer of lack and other unwanted qualities onto woman, "who is required to conceal from the male subject what he cannot know about himself."[12] The classical function of fetishism, her argument continues, is to further alleviate male anxiety about a loss or lack, which is in the final instance his own.

Invisible Adversaries also confronts Freud's account of castration anxiety, but with a special emphasis on the female correlative, so-called "penis envy." As might be expected, parody and humorous bantering set the basic tone in this confrontation. In one sequence the "envy" is thematized in a spoof, when Anna cuts her pubic hair and fashions herself a mustache out of it. This act of defiance is concretized in the subsequent montage, where penis-envy no longer appears as the desire to have something but rather as the wish to be rid of something, as a kind of "role refusal." The montage cuts back and forth between two role-specific activities, that of preparing food, in this case a fish, from live stage to the frying pan, and, parallel to that, the perennial feminine task of cosmetic care and beautification. The rapid crosscutting between these two activities establishes their common denominator as "preparation for consumption," which raises uncomfortable associations. The application of makeup is seen here as the preparation of the object-to-be-looked-at, which is the position Anna has scrupulously avoided throughout by placing herself behind the camera. From this perspective, "envy" has been superceded by refusing her assigned position on the axis of vision, as she is becoming increasingly aware that her ghostly perceptions and her encounters with her doppelgänger are intricately connected to the power that adheres to vision and to the chosen point of view.

In this connection Freud's investigation of the phenomenon of the "uncanny" is highly relevant, since he bases it on aesthetic as well as experiential considerations, and takes E. T. A. Hoffmann's tale "The Sandman" as his point of departure.[13] Hoffmann's tales and *Invisible Adversaries* share a mixture of

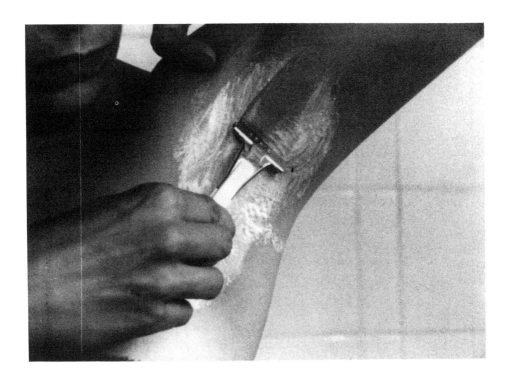

From the "preparation for consumption" sequence

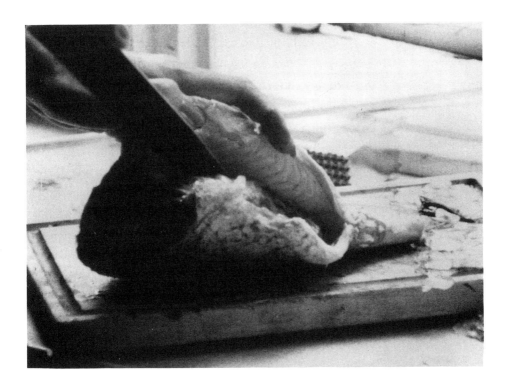

black humor and horror resulting from the animation of objects, the confusion of identities, and the phenomenon of the double.[14] That Freud would draw on dreams and myths to establish the ersatz relation between eyes and the male organ in order to interpret the tale along the lines of oedipal and castration complexes comes as no surprise; nor is it astonishing that, based on this interpretation, the feeling of the uncanny is seen in connection to the psychic mechanism of the return of the repressed and is therefore defined as "that type of the frightening which goes back to the familiar, the intimate of old."[15] What is nevertheless surprising in his account is the repeated and energetic rejection of the importance of Nathaniel's infatuation with a doll to the interpretation of the story.

This rejection is all the more astonishing since it figures centrally in the account of the only precursor of this particular investigation cited by Freud, a certain E. Jentsch. According to the latter's account, the uncanny is predominantly caused by an intellectual uncertainty in the face of phenomena that give cause to doubt whether an apparently living thing is actually alive and conversely, whether an apparently dead object might not be alive after all. While Freud recognizes that this description is especially well suited to explain Hoffmann's "Sandman" tale, he immediately denies its primary importance for this story. Interestingly enough, one of the reasons for doing so is the ironic tone of this passage, in which, Freud contends, the author is poking fun at Nathaniel's overvaluation of his love object. The ironic tone is undeniably present in this passage. However, it is directed at more than Nathaniel's overvaluation of his love object. The irony in this tale is the result of a reverse construction. Before the episode when Nathaniel looks at the doll Olimpia through the binoculars and falls in love with her, he harshly reprimands his fiancée at one of their meetings for trying to persuade him to give up his fantasies about Coppola, calling her at one point: "You damned, lifeless automaton."[16] The major thrust of the irony is clearly directed at Nathaniel's confusion about his love object, the fact that he is infatuated with a mechanical doll and that he calls his caring and concerned fiancée a "lifeless automaton."[17]

Once Freud has established his castration thesis, he finds it necessary to deny Jentsch's observations, this time categorically: " . . . an intellectual uncertainly in Jentsch's sense has nothing to do with this," and again in the next paragraph, "an 'intellectual uncertainty' no longer applies here."[18] The sheer repetitive warding off of the very possibility of intellectual uncertainty in the account of the uncanny points to a blind spot in Freud's interpretative exercise. As if to avoid intellectual uncertainty at all cost, Freud misses the rather emphatic structure of reverse attachments, which consists in calling the live woman an automaton and breathing life into the mechanical doll. A better description of the process of turning woman into a fetish as a result of projection would be hard to come by.[19]

Throughout the film, Anna intuitively touches upon the importance of point of view in her quest for understanding the mechanism of her marginalization. By appropriating it literally in the structure of looking as the one behind the camera rather than as object-to-be-looked-at, she avoids the fetish status that goes hand-in-hand with serving as projection screen for male anxieties. Yet, point of view in its ideological sense seems much harder to detect. It functions so pervasively as to be invisible and seemingly natural. When gender difference is largely subsumed under one gendered identity, the male's genesis of subjecthood, as is the case in Freudian and post-Freudian psychoanalysis, the ideological ramifications of this account are not immediately discernible because they concur with the accepted notion of women's position in society.[20] By repressing the importance of the substitution of the real, material woman in favor of a perfect projection screen, a doll, Freud had placed his theory once again into the service of one (male) story. In this logic of exclusion through incorporation, the dispossession of the annexed "other" causes the splitting of the ego. Regarding the phenomenon of the doppelgänger, Freud describes it in its extreme form in terms of complete confusion of self and other: " . . . so that

Anna's therapist and his Hyksos double

the one possesses the knowledge, feeling and experience of the other, the identification with another person to the point of doubting one's own ego, or replaces one's own ego with that of the other, i.e., ego-doubling, ego-splitting and ego-exchange."[21] Although this is meant to describe a pathological state, it also perfectly characterizes the traditional role expectations for women.

After this long excursion, Anna's Hyksos fantasies appear in a different light. Her question of whether her disturbed state of mind is simply a matter of her subjective perception, or whether the Hyksos have an objective reality of their own cannot be answered in an "either/or" fashion. Instead, Anna comes to the conclusion that the two options are really interdependent. And as if to test this hypothesis with the established arbitrators of mental sanity, she presents her case to a psychologist. As she relates her troublesome double vision to the therapist, she takes his picture, compulsively, only to return to her next session with the developed photos that clearly show the psychologist and his Hyksos double. This lighthearted alignment of the point of view of the camera and Anna's perspective does not preclude a more reflective ending. Anna is going to bed, but dresses herself as if she wants to go on a long hike. As she climbs fully clad between her sheets, an odd spark of hope transpires from her resting place—beds are occasionally symbols of regeneration in Export's visual vocabulary—that she might succeed, after all, in holding her own.

The film ends with a repetition of the camera movements executed at the beginning from inside Anna's apartment to the outside, panning across Vienna's rooftops and back to the inside. Export thinks of this repetition not as closure but as brackets, both to hold together all the heterogeneous elements in the film and to emphasize their very ambiguity and multivalence.

5

Menschenfrauen

Export's second feature-length film, *Menschenfrauen* (Human Women, 1979), picks up where *Invisible Adversaries* left off. Anna's insight into the order of things through her own experience opens up to comparison with other women's lives. Continuity between the films is also maintained in actress Susanne Widl's recurring role as Anna. And again, Peter Weibel is credited with the script as well as the structure of the film, while Valie Export is listed as script collaborator. However, in its concentration on content, the life stories and detailed background of four women, the film departs in conception if not also in style from its predecessor. What was outlined in the first film in structural-skeletal fashion now appears fully fleshed out. While *Invisible Adversaries* translates highly complex personal-emotional material into artistic, distanced visual images, pointing to structural rather than personal positions, *Menschenfrauen* delves into a mode of witnessing that no amount of distancing can diminish in its visceral impact on the viewer. In this sense, *Menschenfrauen* could be considered a "consciousness-raising" film, with many of the elements common to that type of film, such as "true" life stories.

In many ways, the difference between these two features reflects the scope of Export's artistic practice as discussed thus far in her performances, installations, expanded movies, photography, and shorter videotapes. The whole range of shades, from highly abstract and conceptual to graphic and explicitly sensual, is present in her work from the beginning. In spite of the emphasis on "story," *Menschenfrauen* is not devoid of experimental strategies, including several interpolations of her current performance and photographic work. Video is accorded an important place in this film, and it functions in a variety of ways: to retrieve background material from the past; to comment on a present encounter by showing a similar or contrary scene from the past; as memory track, dream, or interior monologue. In every case it signals the points of view of the four women, a veritable quadriga of enunciators whose combined judgment equals the power of the train that finally runs over the man Franz, (Klaus Wildbolz) who has managed to be romantically involved with three and married to one of them. This crisscrossing of temporal and spatial levels prevents identification with any one of the characters, a merciful strategy considering how unbearable their stories are. The stories' claim to "real life" status is ultimately also diminished by strategies that mix biographies and autobiographies in mosaic, if not puzzle, fashion.

The film opens on a flickering video screen as if to introduce the medium itself, which for Export signifies "an essential and symbolic field of action in the art of women of the seventies to explore alternatives to commercial productions and to test the tenuous relation between intimacy and public sphere and between reality and the imagination."[1] Three of the women are introduced on video, showing them in characteristic scenes from their past or in dream sequences. All of the video inserts are uniformly cast in a bluish tint to set them off more effectively from the rest of the film. The first woman, Elisabeth (Renée Felden), appears in a flashback as a child barricaded in a room, desperately trying to tell her mother, who is banging against the door from the outside, that she needs "a room of her own." This reasonable request, reminiscent of Virginia Woolf's reflections on that subject, is here set in the context of an ugly family scene in which mother and son/brother collaborate to tell the girl that only boys have the right to their own rooms.

Gertrud Lehner (Maria Martina) is the second woman, a teacher and the most articulate and intellectual of the group. She is also associated with the performance in this film, based on Export's *I (Beat [It])*. The element borrowed from this event is the lead bandages tied tightly around the performer's wrists, knees, elbows, and ankles. The impact of this performance—which attempted to show the "act of putting the body to an alienated use" and revealing "how little is retained of its identity and how much it is treated and acts as an alien"[2]—is transposed onto the specific character of Gertrud. She is shown wading through a water basin with all the joints in her extremities strapped straight and immobile. Gertrud watches her own performance projected above her typewriter in alternation with a visual track that depicts her past and, at that point, her happy affair with Franz. The sound track to these alternating scenes is equally bifurcated, going back and forth between a poetic text by Export and a TV interview with a young female student who was sentenced to prison for an attempted bank robbery (the TV monitor is situated next to the projection surface above Gertrud's typewriter, where the performance and memory track appear). The overwhelming impression this multilayered montage of sound and images leaves on the viewer is one of isolation and near insurmountable loneliness, a condition also cited as the student's motive for the robbery.

Gertrud's introduction on video is equally estranging and is framed as a dream: she sits fully dressed in a bathtub without water, scrubbing herself meticulously. A big bird sits next to her shoulder on the rim of the bathtub, but Gertrud does not notice it for some time. When she finally does, she bludgeons the bird ferociously and awakens from the dream in horror. Her inability to deal with what seems to be a symbol of her past trauma

Gertrud Lehner

other than by destroying it foreshadows the extreme solution she will finally choose for herself.

Gertrud Lehner's "true life story" illustrates the film's method of composing a narrative mosaic. Her character is the most auto-biographical, as the name Lehner, which is Export's maiden name, deliberately underlines. Also autobiographical is the episode in the courthouse, where the decision is made to take Gertrud's child away and grant custody to her former husband on the grounds that her "library is dangerous" for her child. Weighing most heavily in that decision, however, was her student (i.e., artist) status, which lacked the guarantee of a stable home such as the engineer husband and his new wife could provide. Her antiauthoritarian stance later in her professional career as a teacher, which ends when she slaps the principal in the face, is an autobiographical allusion as well. It is telling that Export substitutes teaching for her own career as an artist. Teaching was the profession of her mother, who grew up and worked in an extremely authoritarian and misogynist environment. The most shocking event of her mother's life came when her father slapped her in the face for dissenting from his opinion even after she had been married. This slap reverberates not only through *Menschenfrauen* but through all of Export's work which, in its caustic criticism of Austrian society, has always been considered an affront to the authorities.

One aspect of the truth-value of these stories functions much like the work done in dreams (*Traumarbeit*). Several persons and their histories are condensed into one, and actions like the slap in the face are displaced in accordance with the principle of wish fulfillment. Gertrud's suicide by electrocution, on the other hand, departs from Export's family history altogether, but is based on an actual death. A newspaper report of suicide by electrocution inspired Export to include the event in the film as part of Gertrud's story. It is an "objet trouvé" with its own claim to truth. Therefore, while the narrative continuity in each of the women's cases is fictive, every one of the building blocks has some relation to an actual event.

The authorial demise inaugurated by modernist writing and finalized by postmodern theoreticians has raised questions in feminist film theory about the status of the female author or director. While the female subject can participate in the "death of the author" by supporting the male's divestiture of his privileges, as far as her own situation is concerned, it is far more important to find a place for the female voice "from which it can speak and be heard, not to strip it of discursive rights."[3] At the same time, the notion of authorship is expanded to include not only the text's materiality, but its narrative and character system as well, and to accept the biographical author, alongside the "author in the text," as one of the many voices spoken.

With regard to the autobiographical dimension in the work of women authors, similar encouragement is appropriate. Feminist research has encountered a condition of repression in women's autobiographical writing parallel to that of women

Gertrud's suicide

writers in general, but exacerbated by the requirements of the genre itself. More than other types of writing, autobiography is predicated upon a male narrative depicting a life story that tends to lead in linear, successive stages to pinnacles of distinction. This opens up a paradox that Domna C. Stanton remarks on when she notes the absence of women in the new realm of auto-biographical criticism, asking: "How could that void be reconciled with the age-old, pervasive decoding of all female writing as autobiographical?"[4] Stanton comes to the conclusion that women's status in the symbolic order was such that they "could not transcend, but only record the concerns of the private self; thus it [the term *autobiographical*] had effectively served to devalue their writing."[5]

At the same time, women writing autobiography are also confronted with the postmodern challenge to the subject representing itself in terms of linguistic, epistemological, or ontological certainty. Again, the question arises whether this challenge applies equally to marginalized subjects whose position is characterized by a lack of certainty and who, through the very process of writing autobiographies, are searching for a way to fortify their sense of self. A number of different strategies emerge out of these contradictory considerations for women who engage in autobiographical work. In her book *A Poetics of Women's Autobiography*, Sidonie Smith discusses three possible ways to proceed. The first instance represents a choice taken most frequently by women who have succeeded in terms of male expectations of public significance. A woman in this position may cast her story "in the culturally compelling plots, ideals of characterization, and speaking posture associated with male or 'human' selfhood."[6] The pitfall of this choice, as Smith points out, is its reinforcement of the ideology of autonomous male identity. And further, the woman who chooses this position must repress the maternal within her in order to attain the symbolic status of the father. As a second alternative, therefore, the female autobiographer "begins to grapple self-consciously with her identity as a woman in patriarchal culture and with her problematic relationship to engendered figures of selfhood."[7] Quite often this stance results in an insistence on the intrinsic difference in female writing, with the attendant danger of essentializing this difference once again. The third option for autobiographical practice, which is also the one Smith seems to embrace, is characterized by the woman autobiographer's refusal to "participate in the fictions at the center of culture, including the fictions of man and woman,"[8] or else use these fictions for her own purposes to subvert the image that patriarchy has created of her. This approach is interested in transforming the boundaries that define center and margin, and to that effect "experiments with alternative languages of self and storytelling."[9]

In as far as Export's authorial voice is enmeshed with the polyphony of the female characters in the diegesis, she is able to take up each one of the three positions described by Smith. In the overall organization of the film's voices, however, her authorial voice is very close to the third option. In the experimental inter-weaving of the women's life stories, their voices support each other to displace whatever image of themselves is forced upon them in the terms of the fictions of the center. Instead they suc-ceed in jointly raising their marginal stories to be central to the narrative in the film.

The director's autobiographical interjections do not repre-sent the "objective," omniscient voice of someone in control behind the narrative because, in all of her films, Export herself steps forward in person to identify, if not the source of speech, at least her personal allegiance with the speaker. Quite often, personal appearances coincide with the performance pieces, which corroborate and comment on the experience of the char-acters. And further, the camera's alignment with the women's point of view, as in the scene with the psychologist in *Invisible Adversaries*, testifies to Export's solidarity with that view. The effect of this identification is twofold. It takes away the aura of author-ity at the same time that it replaces a hierarchical order of enunciation with a field of positions of mutual reinforcement, a "speaking-together," as it were. A different but related situa-tion occurs in *Invisible Adversaries* in the segment entitled "Silent Language," which includes the site of production with Export in control of the technical apparatus. This self-revelation of the director is not an aggressive pushing aside of the actress in order to seize direct control of the diegesis; such a move can be observed in other consciousness-raising films that come to mind, in which the director's didactic impulse takes over. Here, rather, is an attempt to establish a correspondence or identification with the protagonist, who is conceived as the diegetic counter-part of the woman behind the camera. Thus, this strategy rep-resents a doubling or a multiplication the purpose of which is reinforcement.

The third woman introduced in a dreamlike video sequence is Franz's wife Anna, who is seen receiving a gift from him. It is a smart-looking handbag, and Anna expresses grateful appreci-ation. Upon opening the bag, however, she finds to her horror

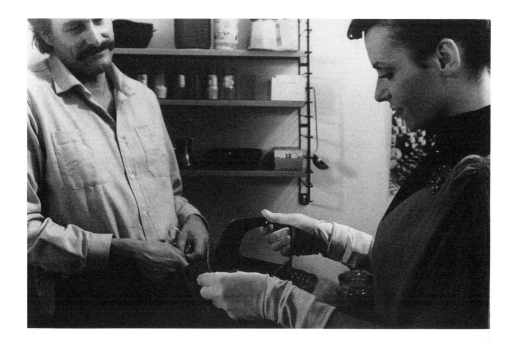

Anna opening her handbag

that it is filled with slime and mud. The appropriateness of the
dream in describing their relationship becomes clear in the following sequences, in which we witness her husband's attempts
to get a date first with Gertrud, then with Elisabeth, and, finally
finding someone receptive to his erotic longings, with Petra
(Christiane von Aster), the fourth woman in his busy schedule.
Foregrounding the comical nature of his crass procedure, the
camera confronts Franz squarely as he runs through his telephone routine, expressing his desire to each woman in identical
terms. Comedy would, indeed, be the proper genre for Franz's
story if it did not feed into the systemic weaknesses of the
women involved, weaknesses which are traced per video and
which are the focus of the film.

What are traced are case histories—fragmentary and incom-
plete to be sure—of the symptoms and developmental background of a disease from which half the population suffers, but
which does not yet have a name. In that sense, the focus of the

film is on experiential data, collected with the unrelenting candor of clinical investigation. Among the four women, Elisabeth is given the most detailed attention with respect to background. Anna is seen primarily in the present and in her difficult relation with her husband. Only one brief scene shows her involved in an altercation with her boss about the appropriateness of her dress at the office. Perhaps because she is older, Elisabeth appears more often in past situations than she does in the present. Her story is essentially that of a battered wife who fights heroically to get custody of her son following divorce from her abusive husband. After a self-sacrificing life of child rearing, she comes to understand that the son has turned out no better than the father when she hears that he has been sentenced to prison for his criminal activities. The most heartbreaking scene in her life—and in the whole film as well—is the moment when her grown son betrays her and aligns himself with the abusive father. In a particularly violent scene, Elisabeth comes close to losing her life at the hands of this man as her son stands nearby simply watching, refusing to come to his mother's aid. The shocking directness of these actions is not mitigated by the different medium (video) used to depict the flashbacks. On the contrary, the ghostly bluish tint and blurred contours increase the immediacy and emotional impact of the scene.

This manner of foregrounding documentary material, fragmented somewhat by avant-garde techniques but not substantially transformed by them (much less than is the case in *Invisible Adversaries*), must ultimately be examined in terms of its correspondence to the demands of the time. *Menschenfrauen* can only be fully appreciated as a conscious product of the feminist movement in Europe and America, which had gained momentum throughout the seventies and had begun to emancipate itself from the tutelage of philosophical, psychological, as well as aesthetic systems of thought whose patriarchal premises and assumptions were considered in need of revision. Helke Sander, a German filmmaker involved in the initial articulation and organization of women artists, addressed the necessity for women's films to transgress what traditionally are considered taboo themes: "It is first of all a shock, to see privacy documented. This is still unusual for the media and has only been made possible by the new women's movement, that is, for approximately ten years now. In order to report, negatively or positively, about the mass phenomenon of the women's movement, it is unavoidable to thematize things that so far have belonged to the protected private sphere."[10]

The obvious objection to this contention is, of course, that the media thrives, and always has, on the very violation of privacy. It is clearly not a matter of privacy per se that is being protected and shielded from the public eye; it is rather the private sphere of ordinary, middle-class women (and, one might add, children as well). The private sphere, as analyzed by Jürgen Habermas in *Structural Changes in the Public Sphere*, is a construct of the classical bourgeoisie, conceived as retreat from their public activities. A place of regeneration and reproduction, it was also considered the only appropriate space for the female members of the family. The protective shield erected around this sphere has always had a double function: in addition to ostensibly providing security from without, it has represented an invisible prison for women and children, who could be harmed both physically and psychologically, with immunity, inside of these ramparts.

That the strict separation of public and private spheres has regulative and normative functions becomes apparent in a scene toward the end of the film. Anna and Petra, both pregnant by Franz and both scorned for it by him, have left him and turned to each other instead for support and affection. Glorying in the power of their newfound sisterhood, they step out for a drink together at an ordinary neighborhood restaurant, both showing the unmistakable signs of advanced pregnancy. For some guests, the mere fact of appearing in public in their "condition" is cause for nagging criticism. Others begin to be alarmed at the incongruity they perceive in the exchange of tenderness between two women who clearly qualify for the category of "wife." Finally, when Anna and Petra, oblivious to the rising tempers around

Anna and Petra—public transgression

them, kiss each other across the table, an explosion erupts: too many taboos have been violated. The entire restaurant is up in arms, demanding that the waiter throw the two women out that instant. The effect of progressive doses of public transgression is not only comical, but also demonstrates the tight norms surrounding the definition of private and public, which in turn preside over the regulation of permissible public behavior in conformity with role expectations.

The irony of the protective zone of the private sphere is that those who are confined to it do not have any privacy within it. While one of the flashbacks shows the mother barring the door to prevent her daughter from leaving the house, its more violent counterpart is the opening scene of the film, which shows the girl barricaded behind the door, trying to defend against the encroachments on her personal sphere. The mother's dictum— that only boys have the right to their own rooms—echoed later in Elisabeth's life when her abusive husband bangs against the door to be let in, claiming that he has a right to her as her husband. Thus, the institution of the private sphere, when examined gender-specifically, turns out to be, indeed, a restful retreat, a haven of regeneration for the contending male returning from his public exploits. For the woman, on the other hand, it represents a double curtailment of freedom. The duties and obligations of the home keep her tied to it and locked into a repetitive routine, while at the same time she becomes constantly and totally accessible to the demands of husband and children, who negate her personal sphere within the home. *Menschenfrauen* has pulled away the lace curtains and sharpened the soft focus on the idyllic hearth to reveal it as one of the more powerful mechanisms in divesting woman of her "self."

Children are implicated in the vicissitudes of domesticity as well. In Export's work, they are never at the center of her considerations, but they are also never quite absent. The enlarged picture of abused children used in *Remote . . . Remote . . .* as backdrop appears again in *Invisible Adversaries* after one of the worst arguments between Anna and Peter and is followed by photos of crashed cars. There, the photo of the children functions in a way similar to the childhood memories of the four women, as a kind of case history, only here it documents the case history of a broken civilization.

In her preface to *Menschenfrauen*, Export writes: "The film shows the psychic and social conditions of women in contemporary society: the breaking apart of old forms of life and the search for new ways of behavior."[11] In its mosaic fashion, the film documents past models of gender interaction from the point of view of their defunct status, as it simultaneously begins to outline a forward-looking perspective. Toward the end of the film, in a freeze-frame tableau, lines are drawn around Gertrud and Elisabeth as victims of the past, whereas Anna and Petra, both younger and carrying the next generation, literally incorporate the future. The scene in the restaurant has shown how unacceptable their solution is to present social sensibilities. Curiously, the attempt to embody the principle of hope in these two figures in the final image of the film caused similar negative reactions among viewers: " . . . even militant women today will find the ending with the two pregnant women bathing their faces in the clean ocean water and entering a future of sisterly love together just plain tacky."[12] By simply presenting a future ideal as present reality, the ending becomes indistinguishable from those ideological constructs that lend an aura of wholesomeness to no matter how sordid a reality. In all of Export's work, this is the only case in which wishful thinking has been allowed to go undetected as the mechanism of a dream. Usually, whatever little hope there is in her films is advanced with great caution, as, for example, at the end of *Invisible Adversaries*, where Anna's meticulous dressing up in a hiking outfit signifies a long and arduous passage. But the ending of *Menschenfrauen* is not the only troubling aspect of the film. Rather, it is a symptom of a more fundamental structural flaw.

The fragmented and multilayered discourse of the image track is countered and to a large extent straitjacketed by the dialogue. Whatever is visually tentative, searching, and probing is short-circuited by an explanatory "political correctness" in the dialogue that is not only blunt and obtrusive but ultimately undermines what the film sets out to do. This excessively obvious spelling out of everything is also carried over into character depiction. While, for example, Franz's initial spiel on the phone—trying to charm women but sounding like a broken record—is a felicitous introduction in that it sets the scene and describes his person, all subsequent elaborations on this theme are counterproductive. When we follow on the trail of Franz's vast sexual appetite, watching him simultaneously court Elisabeth and reject the two women he has recently impregnated, or when we are treated to a montage of his split personality in his relation to Anna, our point of view is gradually reversed. As Export pathologizes his monstrous behavior, Franz gains in stature through sheer fascination. The women, on the contrary, lose what little interest they initially held as the victims in this sordid story. Given the exaggerated and fairly transparent nature of Franz's soap opera, it is hard not to add insult to injury and blame the women for putting up with him for so long.

Fortunately, the film is not entirely destroyed by the script's mistaken zealousness, which at times has more to do with the application of the latest ideas than with a true concern for women. What saves *Menschenfrauen* are its strong images, its poetic passages, and its actresses. Nevertheless, it is highly ironic, to say the least, that Export's ostensibly most feminist film turns, upon closer inspection, around the staging of the male ego. Even Franz's comical death cannot obliterate this impression, since it happens much too late in the film. Neither is there much consolation in the belated insight on Anna's part that women are fully human only when they no longer have to become mothers. And finally, the epitaph "We must create a human society in which motherhood does not restrict woman in her creativity and determination" oddly drifts in the air, not having been anchored to any particular discussion in the film except perhaps to grant leave without guilt to Franz.

Menschenfrauen remains a valuable document of the feminist concern with consciousness-raising in the seventies. The testimonial bluntness that frequently characterizes the products of this genre is countered in Export's case by her way of fragmenting the individual women's life stories and weaving them into a coalition of voices. Export's own voice emerges out of the interstices of this text, giving expression to biographical content at the same time that she supports the position of other women in a larger political framework.

6

The Practice of Love

M ade in the decade of postfeminism, Export's third feature film, *Die Praxis der Liebe* (The Practice of Love,
1984), once again takes stock of the implications of the times for
women as well as for art. Gone are the sisterly embraces and life-
sized stories of the late seventies; the professional woman
answering to no one but herself has replaced all that. In keeping with her new status, she not only has a new first name, but
a surname as well. Judith Wiener (Adelheid Arndt), a journalist
in her late twenties with a public workplace, office, boss, and
colleagues she is attached to, has come a long way, it seems, from
the all-purpose "Annas" standing for all women. At first sight
Judith has arrived, successful and independent in her profession, and in her private life dividing time between two admiring
lovers. So much mysterious good fortune calls for an investigation, it would seem. Perhaps it is precisely that unconscious
incredulity that drives Judith to look beneath the surface of the
world that surrounds her. What she finds there shatters not only
her emotional equilibrium, but her social and professional relation to the world as well. In fact, the continuity and interconnectedness between her private realm and her public activity

moves the film story, which could be described as a political thriller, in a direction that is specifically interesting to women.

The traditional thriller's convention of the private eye takes on a whole network of meanings in *The Practice of Love*. This position, which is traditionally assigned to the male hero or antihero, is here occupied by a female character. Because of the inclusion of the private sphere in the criminal investigation, the conventions of film noir are pertinent here. According to these conventions, the male investigator gets sidetracked from solving the crime by his private concerns, usually his attraction to the female protagonist in the story, who is often implicated in the crime. Judith's lover is involved in the crime as well, and it is expected of her, as the woman, that she subordinate her professional "ambitiousness" to the vicissitudes of their love affair. By refusing this role, Judith is either the mirror opposite of the film noir antihero, or perhaps just a positive view of the much feared femme fatale. Her insistence is tenacious, and she does succeed in uncovering the crime. Yet, in another deviation from the convention, the perpetrators and the administrators of the law turn out to be in secret agreement, allowing the criminals to go free in the end, while the investigator runs for her life.

The reversal of the structure of looking, already a project for Anna in *Invisible Adversaries*, is completed in this feature. The woman is not only behind the camera, but, as the tradition of the private eye prescribes, is in control of the film narrative as well. It is through Judith's progressive piecing together of information—partly collected in painstaking research and partly coming to her by chance—that the viewer begins to understand the extent of the corruption surrounding her. But Judith discovers more than political corruption. She also comes to understand that the possibility of reversing the structure of looking is limited at best, and that her detective activities are monitored by a system of surveillance far superior to her efforts.

The plot is loosely based on an actual arms smuggling scandal in contemporary Austria that was finally prosecuted in the so-called Proksch Affair (after the name of the key dealer) five years

Judith within the structure of looking

after the film premiered. Austria's neutral status prohibits the production, trade, or sale of weapons to any nation, especially if that nation is at war. Media reports and pictures of Austrian-made tanks and weapons inspired the basic story of an illegal deal involving Austrian weapons and Algerian buyers. The details of the transaction are left largely unarticulated, and instead the emphasis is on Judith's efforts to solve the crime, in the course of which she winds up at her own doorstep. One of the dealers, Dr. Alfons Schlögel (Rudiger Vogler), happens to be Judith's lover. This coincidence represents another example of the interpenetration of the public and private spheres. A similar constellation applies to her other lover, Dr. Joseph Fischoff (Hagnot Elischka), a psychiatrist whose public representation as pillar of the psychoanalytic establishment stands in stark contrast to his inept handling of his own psychic and emotional affairs.

The linkage of public and private spheres, a major concern in all of Export's work, is followed through on a new level in *The Practice of Love*. Here the two spheres have been more or less collapsed in the persons of Judith's amorous choices. On the narrative level, Judith's most private and intimate life not only becomes affected by the public activities of her lovers, but directly exerts its own reciprocal force upon their status. This is particularly apparent in her relation to the arms dealer, Dr. Schlögel. What the film first establishes as a tender and sensuous love affair—some of the most beautiful and cinematically most exciting passages go into this thematic—instantly turns into bitter antagonism once Judith has procured enough evidence of Schlögel's involvement in the smuggling deals and challenges him openly about his activities. His attempt to stem her investigations takes the shape of ridiculing her participation in the public sphere, telling her that she does not have enough information or knowledge of the dangerous ramifications of this criminal affair. How right he is, despite his manipulative intentions, becomes clear to Judith at the conclusion of her detective work. Equipped with sufficient evidence to demonstrate that a subway accident that claimed the life of a young man was really a murder perpetrated by members of the ring of arms dealers, she naively presents her case to members of the governmental agency with jurisdiction over the crime. To her great consternation, however, she learns that the information is not welcome, recognizing the agency's tacit complicity with and possible involvement in the illegal arms dealing affair.

Dr. Schlögel's request that Judith drop her investigations lest they destroy their relationship is tantamount to the suggestion that women have no moral obligation other than supporting their men in whatever they happen to be doing. Freud's elaborate psychoanalytical testimony concerning women's lack of moral fiber might have been undercut by a simple reference to this traditional prohibition against a woman's exercising her moral judgment in public. Schlögel's sarcastic remark about Judith's "moral stories of abused women and children" is not only directed at Judith's activities (we only see her working on a story on peep shows) but represents a very clear autobiographical reference to Export's experience with the critical reception of

Menschenfrauen. Morality in the hands of women very quickly becomes an object of ridicule.

The depictions of male and female characters in *The Practice of Love* are almost inversely proportionate. To the degree that Judith has become more of a differentiated individual, thanks to her gain in subjecthood, the two male characters have lost ground with respect to rounded accounts of their personae, their motivation, and their social interaction. Instead, they function as ciphers; that is, their characterization is paradigmatic for certain aspects of society, selected to shed light on Judith's position within it. They represent the two kinds of terror—the public and the private—Judith is embroiled in and is struggling to overcome. Ironically, her detective activity opens only her own eyes to an unsavory world, and she pays a high price for this enlightenment. As the soft focus on her love affairs and on her professional success is dispelled bit by bit by her keen and fearless perseverance, the strength that seemed to adhere to these two spheres of her life is shown to be an illusion.

The cipher status of Dr. Schlögel's character is very effective in foregrounding the discontinuity between Judith's public and private life and, further, in linking this discontinuity to a separate, superimposed order of violence and surveillance that seems to be pervasive. Any detailed attention to Schlögel's individual personality or psyche would have detracted from the fact that this order is larger than he is and that once he has taken up a certain position within it, his actions are also circumscribed by it. As it is, Schlögel is clearly under the same threat of violent annihilation that has already claimed the life of his younger partner, should he not deliver his part of the bargain. This group of criminals also shatters Judith's life at the end, metaphorically depicted in the destruction of her apartment. Her hasty departure, leaving her job, her friends, and the city with all its social contacts to go into exile, culminates in the vertiginous fall, down the back stairs, of something that at first seems to have been Judith. But when the shattered pieces are deciphered, it turns out to be the film's title substituting for her. Only when we hear, over the film's end credits, the voice of an airport announcer calling out an airline number for a Chicago flight, can we assume that Judith is safe.

These incidences of actual and suggested violence are therefore not entirely reducible to any one character or even gender, let alone the popular belief in "good and bad guys." They are linked instead to one of Judith's more startling lines, in which she states that "the human bloodbath itself . . . it is our God." If, as Hannah Arendt claimed, "the practice of violence, like all action, changes the world, but the most probable change is to a more violent world,"[1] the involvement of the "practice of love" in this vortex of violence calls for closer critical scrutiny of the very anatomy of love. In *The Practice of Love*, the implication of the relations between the sexes in the general social fabric of destructiveness (which could be observed in *Invisible Adversaries* and went on record in the form of life stories in *Menschenfrauen*), is placed in the crucible of a dialectical scrutiny probing equally into the impact of external violence on a love relation and into the effect of psychic violence on the very possibility of such a relation (or any social relation, for that matter). While the first instance is played out in Judith's interaction with Dr. Schlögel, the latter finds its focus in her love for Joseph Fishoff.

In her attempt to articulate the dynamics of psychic violence, Export does not concentrate, as she did to some extent in *Menschenfrauen*, on the male perpetrator and the female victim. Here, the emphasis is on the dynamics itself, a choreography of repercussions and shifting positions. The volatility of Joseph and Judith's amorous interaction can trigger violently destructive responses depending on a vast array of external impingements. It is precisely this choreography of positions that allows the opening of the film—an elaborate peep show sequence—to reflect on this most intimate relation between Judith and Joseph.

The film's opening shot focuses on a peep show establishment located in a busy city street. Judith is interviewing a male passerby on his opinions about such places. His view that all of these practices would be just fine if the girls stayed "clean," by which he means that they should cater only to bachelors and not to married men, hardly comes as a surprise to Judith. The feebleness of this tired tradition of laying not only the moral burden but also the blame on the women becomes apparent as soon as Judith enters the "inner sanctum" of the establishment. We see her behind her camera looking intently through her lens and in seeming amusement setting the camera aside as she fixes her gaze on one particular point. The reverse shot reveals the face of a man peering through a small window which is just lighting up, presumably a signal that he has paid his fee. The reflection of the woman on display is visible below the window in a mirror. Only a later shot, a quasi-omniscient authorial view from a high angle, shows the naked woman directly at the center of a room lined with windows, the faces of men pressed against the panes. Judith, with her camera in hand, stands arm's length from the woman. This reversal of the traditional camera eye/male gaze alignment, placing the camera in a woman's hands at the interior of the space on which all the male gazes converge, not only defies and throws back the aggression of that gaze but also introduces another emotion, quite different in temperament. It first appears in Judith's face as she sets her camera aside to take stock of the little windows and their occupants lining the wall around her, and can best be described as "bemused compassion."

This sentiment enables Judith to switch positions and to move back and forth between the point of view of the woman on display and that of the male viewers. In one such point-of-view reversal, the camera (this time not identified as Judith's but simply assumed to be so because of her absence in the center), is positioned inside one of the "visitor's" cubicles and is recording not just the woman's performance but the tactile frustration of the voyeur as well, as his hand (sole visual representative of his persona) lovingly and pathetically traces the woman's body's outline on the window. The distance created by this staggering of viewpoints, as well as by Judith's position switches, allows the spectators to extricate themselves from identification with either the male voyeur or the woman on display. Instead, a third position arises, which corresponds to Judith's insight into the nature of both these poles without adopting either one. From this vantage point, there are neither victims nor oppressors. This perspective is made poignantly clear when Judith, at the end of her stay in the peep show, interviews the women and asks whether any of them would work there if the men were actually able to touch them. The women's explanation—that they enjoy caressing their own bodies in the manner prescribed by their job, but would not consider working there if the men could touch them— counteracts both the assumption that their actions have any bearing on the choice of their clients (or on selecting them by marital status), as well as any simple notion of the unilateral exploitation of their bodies. The stance of bemused compassion includes both viewers and viewed in a universe of obscenity, whose bottom line may be pleasure, but most certainly is business.

Judith gives words to this insight at the conclusion to her peep show report, when she speaks into a microphone in front of her camera team just outside of the porn shop: "The persons who profit from pornography can be found among the top businessmen. It is they who profit from their own gender's sexual distress and lust for obscenities. The language of pornography is a dark one, echoing in the catacombs of society. In this mechanical ballet the women are but objects, display items." The entry of a Black man at the words, "the language of pornography is a dark one," points to a link between the exploitation of sexuality and that of race, and beyond that comments ironically on the role of language in that exploitation. Predictably, the tape is turned down by the television station she tries to sell it to later, on the grounds that it does not fit into the station's programming or standards. A definitive limit to the reversal, or rather dispersal, of the structure of looking has been reached.

The treatment of Judith's relation with Joseph is similarly placed outside an explicit point-of-view alignment with either partner. While on the whole, the film's point of view coincides with Judith's, when it comes to the intimate dynamics of their interaction, it discreetly steps aside to let each party speak for her- or himself. At the same time, the authorial view occasionally comments in its own bemused way, be it only in the particulars of the framing of their encounters. A humorous example of this occurs at their meeting at the hospital, just after Judith returns from her trip to Hamburg, where she had worked on her peep show report. As she enters his office, Joseph is in the process of watching a film dealing with modern medicine's latest insights on epilepsy. It shows a patient in the throes of a fit, strapped to a bed and completely wired, presumably to different measuring instruments. Over the speaker's observation that epilepsy is no longer considered a singular sickness but rather a syndrome with more or less intense patterns of fits, the two lovers, delighted at their reunion, rush into each others arms, embracing at the exact point at which the projection beam traverses the room, so that their faces become the screen for a brief moment, identifying them with the writhing victim of an epileptic fit. The technique hails from Export's early expanded movies, such as *Cutting*, where the human body is frequently used as screen. Here it has a narrative, commenting function that sets the scene for the couple's meeting later that day.

Twice the narrative circles around the inner core of their relationship, their intimate sphere, where seemingly only private emotions rule. And twice the encounter ends in the kind of epileptic fit portrayed previously on film, causing great damage to internal and external spaces. The emotional devastation resulting from their sexual jealousies, their nagging and verbal abuses, translates quite automatically into the real physical devastation of the apartment as objects are turned into missiles and messengers of frustration. It is mainly Judith who externalizes internal states, taking it one step further by including the filmic material in the general battle. One of her furious arm movements becomes engraved in a blazing trail onto the film strip itself, crossing through the entire middle section of the frame.

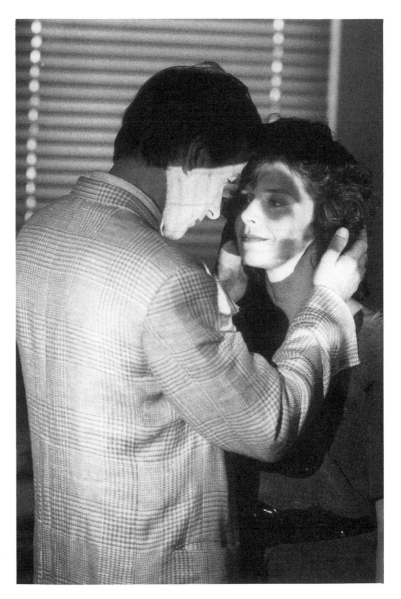

Judith and Joseph as screen

Originally designed to call attention to the materiality of the film medium under the auspices of Expanded Cinema, the implementation of this technique at this point in the film narrative opens onto a number of speculations. In as far as Judith's gesture foregrounds the film's materiality, a parallel exists between the body of the film and her body. The violent slashing motion of her arm in effect crosses out the film text, out of the scene from which she wants to extricate herself. And further, the filmmaker's intervention on a metanarrative level, her technical assistance in crossing out the text, is yet another instance of Export's frequent identification with her female protagonists and characters. In this case the alliance is not, as is frequently the case, based on point of view, but rather on putting the body into play, that is, forming an alliance between the bodies of the film, of the protagonist, and of the filmmaker.

During this entire encounter, there is division on the level of enunciation. While Joseph explodes in verbal hemorrhages, venting his jealous suspicions, Judith remains almost completely silent, mockingly watching his futile efforts to give words to the confusion of his emotions. At one point, she holds a tape recorder up to him to record his ungenerous bickering and then plays the tape back to him to make her point. Her own reaction to their strife is expressed almost exclusively through gestures and actions. These become a more truthful statement of what is

Judith slashes the film and the film text

ailing them, much in the manner of the anxious lover put under scrutiny by Roland Barthes: "I can do everything with my language, *but not with my body*. What I hide by my language, my body utters."[2] As long as Judith is willing to take on that mute and truthful body-wrenching labor, a certain amount of catharsis is guaranteed, and the stormy exchange subsides in favor of fervent lovemaking.

Perhaps this resolution is further aided by Judith's acting out the scenario of the master–slave dialectic. In her reading of Plato's *Phaedrus*, Julia Kristeva has identified this dialectic as "at the basis of the relationship between lover and loved one,"[3] even in the psychic space of its "Platonic," spiritual version. Judith gets down on the floor and begins to act like a dog, licking the floor and finally nipping Joseph in the ankle; his initial anger dissolves very quickly, and he is suddenly eager to reverse the situation, to be her dog, her watchdog, in order to protect her, as he puts it. The scene immediately recalls one of Export's earliest street actions with Peter Weibel, *Aus der Mappe der Hundigkeit* (From the Portfolio of Doggedness), in which she leads Weibel on a leash through Vienna like a dog. What in the sixties was a challenge to the notion of domination in traditional male–female relationships appears in *The Practice of Love* as the bottom line of the anxiety that accompanies amorous attachments. The reversal enacted by Joseph is not so much a solution to the problem as it is an expression of relief that Judith was able to put her finger on his woes.

A true reversal, or better, a genuine equilibrium in relational give-and-take might have been achieved in the second, equally stormy encounter. It is a symmetrical companion piece to the first, almost its mirror image. This time it is Judith who verbalizes her discontent with Joseph's insistence on remaining married while professing to love her. Amid the violent upheaval of her jealous emotions, she is nevertheless able to wonder why it is so hard for her to accept this state of affairs, since after all, she herself is involved with another man. In the face of her distress, Joseph, however, only exacerbates the situation by insisting on his "freedom" even more pointedly. Without anyone to assist her as she had assisted Joseph—i.e., by physically acting out anxiety—Judith is left to work through this emotional extremity on her own. Significantly, the encounter does not end in a reunion, but in a stalemate. And in the following sequence, Judith descends alone into those recesses of her soul where eroticism touches on violence and the death drive is depicted in a dreamlike passage reminiscent of Surrealist film practices. Judith rides a bike through the eerily deserted city; behind her a heavy gate with the inscription "defenseless" (*wehrlos*) crashes shut. On her course, she encounters signs of destruction, but oddly enough not visual images of horror, as might be expected in the context of a ride that looks very much like a journey into the unconscious; instead she finds herself surrounded by a veritable forest of written signs, as if to acknowledge Lacan's observation that the unconscious is structured like a language. At first these signs appear in the form of newspaper pages blown about in the street and at one point pasted up in huge format over half of a house front. Geometric

Signs of Judith's unconscious

signs that look like the letters of a phantasmatic alphabet litter the walls of houses until a large poster with the inscription "the worst crime ever committed" ("*die schrecklichste Bluttat die es je gab*") appears, succeeded by a memento on the pavement of St. Stephan's square, "16-year-old student died."

At the furthest recess of Judith's descent, however, images finally take on the difficult task of confronting the deepest, most murderous aggression she harbors. Cycling around a corner of the cathedral, Judith runs head on into a visibly pregnant woman pushing a pram, who on closer inspection turns out to be Joseph's wife. The poor woman's terrified behavior and frantic attempt to escape from Judith suggests that the subsequent murder of the woman is perpetrated by Judith, even though she is not shown with a gun. This ambiguity about the origin of the gunshots echoes the ambiguity of Judith's state of mind and marks the end of this sequence. The camera, in a reverse shot, comes to rest on Judith's distraught face. The sound of the shooting, however, is carried over into the next sequence, the raid of a house that apparently serves as a weapons arsenal. In turn, this sequence blends into a series of documentary clippings portraying war scenes of extraordinary violence and cruelty.

By mounting these three sequences together in a continuum, Export establishes the connection between psychic and political, private and public violence that is crucial to her investigation into the practice of love. Judith's understanding of the apotheosis of the "human bloodbath" is here traced to the seed of it in every individual, including herself. And thus, while free from crudely moral or moralizing tendencies, *The Practice of Love* nevertheless raises the question of whether, aside from any personal (or even gender) blame to be meted out, all of Western civilization might not have taken a wrong turn at some point. Even Freud's postulation of an original separate, aggressive, and destructive drive in mankind does not account for the totalizing effect depicted by Export not only in *The Practice of Love* but in her other two feature films as well, most prominently in *Invisible Adversaries*, where this effect is experienced by Anna as a takeover from outer space. Perhaps it is precisely this escalation of violence in public and private life that has prompted recent interpretations of Freud's principle of Eros and Thanatos as totally irreconcilable, a view which "works very much to the advantage of the principle of Thanatos itself, since of course Thanatos is itself the principle of irreconcilability."[4] From this rather pessimistic perspective, the eventual absorption of life forces by the death drive seems inevitable. Freud himself, while seeing no cause for euphoria with regard to human nature and civilization, nevertheless chose a more balanced and, above all, more historical approach to the problem:

> Mankind has progressed in the domination of natural forces to a point where it can, with their help, exterminate itself to the last man. They know that, which explains a good portion of their current unrest, unhappiness and mood of anxiety. But now it is to be expected, that the other of the two 'heavenly forces,' eternal Eros, will strain to get the upper hand in the battle with his equally immortal opponent.[5]

Freud's differentiation between separate drives, which he defined in opposition to C. G. Jung's notion of a unitary libido, does not necessarily point to the dominance of Thanatos. His view is far more dialectical when he stresses both their collaboration and their oppositionality: "Thus next to Eros there is a death drive; the phenomena of life could be explained through the joint and contradictory efforts of the two."[6]

Why then has our civilization grown so unbalanced, the film seems to ask insistently, and what are the mechanisms that favor aggression and destruction? One scene in particular probes into this failure of love. It occurs toward the end of the film, summing up, as it were, Judith's disillusionment with her various attempts at closeness and loving contact. Standing alone in her studio, she faces three video cameras and addresses Joseph, who is only visible on the monitors behind her, while he challenges and defies her impassioned queries:

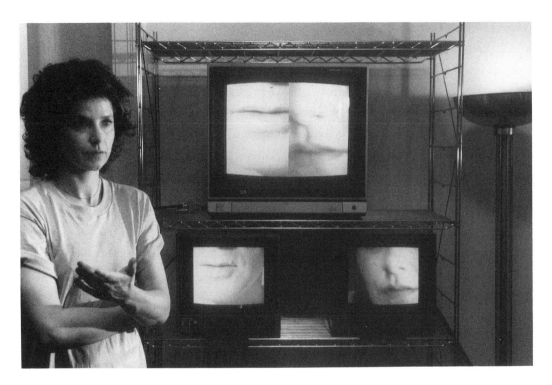

Judith addresses Joseph via video monitors

JUDITH: I was wishing you would be the guardian of my hopes. I was longing to feel beautiful, intelligent, spontaneous, enthusiastic with you. I thought I had found that which I believed to have strengthened me.

JOSEPH: You are an egotist.

JUDITH: Am I an egotist if I say that I need this strength? If I have enough I can give some back to you. Or do you want this mediocrity of living side by side . . . ?

JOSEPH: You are without limits; you don't want to acknowledge any limits. We should keep more distance, respect authority better.

JUDITH: I know you ask for more indifference, but you say distance and you mean blurred circumstances.

JOSEPH: A less urgent desire to own the other, less observation.

JUDITH: So you become inaccessible, can indulge in your weaknesses. . . .[7]

What Judith mourns in this passage is not only the failed relationship as such, but her specific expectations for it as a potential source of pleasure. In her book *The Bonds of Love*, Jessica

Benjamin examines this very expectation in the light of various trends in psychoanalysis and comes to the conclusion that the whole notion of pleasure "had gotten lost in the transition from drive theory to ego psychology."[8] From this perspective, Joseph's insistence on distance corresponds to the classic psychoanalytic viewpoint that "did not see differentiation as a balance, but as a process of disentanglement. Thus it cast experiences of union, merger, and self–other harmony as regressive opposites to differentiation and self–other distinction."[9] Judith's hopes for feeling "beautiful, intelligent, spontaneous, enthusiastic" *with* her partner are closer to Benjamin's alternative, proposed in her theory of intersubjectivity, which is based on mutual recognition and a capacity to keep a balance between separation and connectedness. The endorsement and validation of separateness, which in its extreme version, as Benjamin points out, "pathologized the sensation of love,"[10] has no doubt taken its toll in the balance of the battle between "eternal Eros" and the forces of destruction.

The powerful image of Judith, surrounded by her video equipment and confronting the absent Joseph, brings the film's many references to the technology of communication to a surprising conclusion. In many ways, the scene stands in contradistinction to the way technology is played out in the rest of the film. Predicated upon the metaphor of the peep show, the social exchange involving technological apparatuses is strictly a one-way proposition. People do not communicate; they are being watched. Camera eyes proliferate in subways, in ordinary street traffic, making everyone's moves readable on monitors located elsewhere. Yet, when it comes to reaching a friend by telephone, frustration prevails: broken-down equipment, unwilling owners, queues at phone booths make the effort to communicate exorbitant in proportion to its end.

Locked into these integrated circuits of control and surveillance, Judith takes seriously the challenging question posed in one of Joseph's seminars: "What technological species is mankind a part of?" The argument continues that this new question challenges a more ancient one, which had investigated "how and in which form is cognition of the responsibilities and obligations of mankind possible." Judith's interest in the first question, however, does not preclude her allegiance to the second position. While all of the tools Judith depends on in her trade are advanced technological instruments, she is not at their mercy. On the contrary, it is precisely her intimate knowledge of this equipment that enables her to exercise her responsibility as a journalist and as a citizen. Similarly, the confrontation between Judith and Joseph, via her video cameras and monitors, eclipses all of her personal encounters with him in the sheer honesty and poetic quality of her expression. What is at stake is not technology, but the use we make of it: "The machine is us, our processes, an aspect of our embodiment. We can be responsible for machines; they do not dominate or threaten us. We are responsible for boundaries; we are they."[11] By placing her equipment at the disposal of her resolute search for love and her equally intense attempt to prevent the destructive forces involved in the arms deals from going forward, Judith points not only to the interconnectedness of these two concerns but also to the inextricability of her mental and physical resources and their prosthetic offspring, *techne*.

7

Syntagma

After the completion of two feature films and before embarking on the third, Export returned once again to a purely experimental mode when she made *Syntagma* (1983) a 16 mm multimedia film. This short film (twenty minutes) consolidates not only the great variety of avant-garde techniques accumulated over two decades of work in Expanded Cinema, video, and photography, but also the insights gleaned from her body work in performances, actions, and installations. At the same time, feminism both as methodology and personal experiential stance, which had left an indelible mark on Export's art during the 1970s, continued to be the single most important impulse and thematic source in her work in the 1980s.

The reappropriation of the female body from its perceived sense of alienation has been at the forefront of Export's feminist concerns. The female body, thus perceived, is in fragments, split and ruined, lacking cohesion, "the site not only of an anatomical but of discursive lack."[1] The striking insistence in *Syntagma* on the fragmented body of the woman, mute for the most part, has a twofold and seemingly contradictory impact. Fragmentation first appears to be the repetition of a trauma until, finally, its frenetic pace turns into deliberate composition. In the traumatic sense, fragmentation reflects the epitome of objectification, an itemization of the goods: arms, legs, shoulders, breasts, faces, the depersonalized review of the chattel's grade. This commodity's exchange value for society is nothing less, according to Lévi-Strauss, than its very survival. Yet if a Marxist analysis of the commodity could be applied seamlessly to the position of women in patriarchal society, then Luce Irigaray's notion of the "goods getting together" ironically would be an integral part of the system, falling under the rubric of the "fetishism of commodities," rather than an oppositional feminist strategy. The point is that while women may be objectified, they do not therefore necessarily become objects. It is cynical, to say the least, to take ideology at face value. What is needed is the kind of "double focus"[2] that involves the acknowledgment of what is, but also an image of what could be different—or at the very least, a recognition of the well-known fact that women are not just merchandise, but also consumers. Regarding this latter proposition, Mary Ann Doane observes that the contradiction is only apparent, and that it "involves rethinking the absoluteness of the dichotomy between subject and object which informs much feminist thinking and analyzing the ways in which the woman is encouraged to actively participate in her own oppression."[3]

The body is perhaps the best arena in which to carry on this rethinking and analyzing. It is the meeting ground of subject and object or, to quote R. D. Laing's *The Divided Self* (from *Syntagma*): "The body clearly takes a position between me and the world. On the one hand this body is the center of my world and on the other it is the object in the world of the others." Placed into a feminist context, or rather into a feminist film text, these words take on added meanings, ranging from the narcissistic self-referentiality typical of confined states to the familiar equation of woman and commodity. Just how much these two positions are sides of the same coin remains to be investigated. Both depend on the unbridgeable gap between

Fragmented woman

subject and object. In an effort to decrease this gap, *Syntagma*, like so much of Export's work in the 1960s and 1970s, postulates an expansive body, one that can escape confinement and animate—that is, endow with proper motion—its interaction with the world.

Breaking through confinements is the expansive body's constant preoccupation. *Syntagma* establishes this thematic in the first sequence of images which, in what looks like a birth, shows two hands gradually forcing their way through two parallel running film strips. Once out in the open and in view, the hands communicate the title of the film using sign language. Birth is metaphorically invoked again—designating the crossover between subject and object—in the woman's escalator ride from the underground station, the womb of the city, to the surface and into the city's bustle. For Export the city is both feminine and masculine (traditionally speaking), feminine in its housing, sheltering, and protecting of life, masculine in its traffic, commerce, and communication. There is, however, a more powerful reason for considering the city as doubly gendered. One of the stories in Italo Calvino's book *Le città invisibili* relates how the city of Zobeide was founded exactly on that site where several men, pursuing the same dream, encountered each other. The site corresponded to the place where they lost the object of their desire, a woman, out of sight. This story suggests that "the city constitutes itself through the attempt to lend duration to the desire expressed in their dream . . . as the site of absence of the woman in whose place a league of men gather together, bound to each other through the lack of the feminine."[4]

In Export's sequel to this story, the absent woman henceforth haunts the discontented citizenry of this civilization. In one particular sequence in *Syntagma*, the woman's image appears in the side mirrors of cars without ever referring to her actual presence in this sequence. Yet, the relation of woman to the city need not be entirely negative: "if the city can exclude women, as a cultural community in which men alone transact business, govern the nation, and enforce laws, it can also free women for the first time from their isolation in the private home."[5] If Export's relation to the urban environment has been a problematic one from the beginning, this has been accepted as

VALIE EXPORT

Escalator ride; birth into the city bustle

a challenge in her work instead of avoided as foregone con-
clusive defeat.

Motion is the expansive body's basic means of expression. The
freedom to move unencumbered through space, to determine
one's own movement in relation to the world of objects has,
like free speech, long been recognized as every person's inalien-
able right. Yet the quality of speech and the quality of movement
remain unspecified. What does it avail anyone to speak but not
to be heard, or worse, to be considered mad? And likewise, what
is the good of motion if it does not correspond to the mover's
design? It is "the way of the hysteric, of experiencing one's body
(or 'piece of life') set in motion apart from one's own intentions."[6] In *Syntagma* motion is scrutinized and differentiated.
In the inner sanctum, the traditional locus assigned to woman,
the house, the home, her motion resembles that of Rilke's captive
panther pacing back and forth behind bars. It is motion that

The "absent" woman's image in the side mirror

betrays potential strength, pent-up explosive energy that reaches a pitch of accelerated frenzy.

Entrapment in this locus is particularly virulent, as becomes clear in a sequence involving the woman's photographed body parts embedded in a sheet. Several codes and connotations in this sequence work together to create a sense of excruciating pain. Photographs of segments of the woman's body are placed on a sheet and partially draped with it so that a crease formed by the sheet cuts through the already fragmented body of the woman. These fragmented fragments are accompanied by a sound track that very such resembles a staple gun going off or a nail being hammered every time a new photograph is placed on the sheet. The significance of beds and sheets, distilled from Export's earlier performance work, has birth and death connotations but focuses in this sequence specifically on the burden patriarchal society places on women as a result of their biological function. In a later repetition of this sequence, the sheet is removed. This choice, and the fact that the black-and-white photographs are doubled by identical images on color film in warm skin tones (a technique rehearsed in *Ontological Leap*), are strategies of reappropriating the woman's body. In the careful differentiation and articulation between representations in the film, video, photography, and other media within the context of this film, photography ranks as the most immobilizing and objectifying. Doubling photographic images with identical film images metaphorically restores mobility.

Beyond this most private sphere, in the outer circle of public communication and transportation, motion undergoes incisive change. The shot that characterizes this sphere and is repeated six times in the course of the film is the layered multimedia collage of women's feet walking up and down a staircase. In what looks at first like an homage to Duchamp's famous celebration of movement, *Nude Descending a Staircase*, it is precisely the aspect of movement that cannot be reproduced statically—duration—that in *Syntagma* turns celebration into frustration. The last rather long sequence of shots of women's feet on stairs begins rather playfully, superimposing not only different medial representations but also a multiplicity of codes—the bare foot and the femininely coded foot in high heels. Soon repetition turns into tedium as the last low-angle shots of this sequence endow the foot with an almost animalistic quality, another step down the road to objectification: woman as the beast of burden. This progression reaches its nadir (in the context of the urban environment) in a piece that refers back to the *Body Configurations in Architecture* of the 1970s. The woman lies face down beside a staircase fitted into an opening in the wall; she literally fills

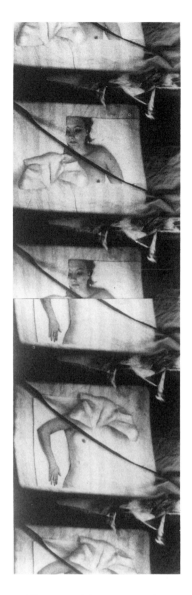

Photographic segmentation

in the gap. The triangular shape of the staircase and a crying baby on the sound track powerfully underline the biological overdetermination of women's identity in patriarchal society. The fact that the filmmaker chooses this passage to introduce herself, to place herself—in another multimedia collage—in exactly the same position as the prone woman (again a film and photography superimposition) signals a significant identification. Another subject–object gap is being bridged in the woman artist's embrace of the woman-as-object dilemma. This subject–object crossover is perhaps the most crucial for feminism.

The exact exploration of velocity and space and of the polarity of masculine construction and feminine dissolution give the film a certain structuralist appearance. Again and again, however, these polarities are cut through with the boldest of cinematic strategies. Breaking away from the frustrating movement of the woman's feet, the camera ascends to the top of the staircase, surveying the flight of stairs descending on both sides; it describes a 360-degree circle in the middle of a large city square, allowing the body (that is, the body of the filmmaker) full and unobstructed vision and motion in all directions. Such counter-movements effectively halt frenetic repetition, introducing a mode of action more akin to exercising or rehearsing a new role, as the place of fragmentation turns into a building site. This use of fragmentation as a place of construction, an open-ended process of reshaping women's lives, is Export's answer to its traumatic repetitiveness.

Fragmentation, both hailed and decried in the modernism debates half a century ago in Russia and Central Europe, is borne out in *Syntagma* to the full extent of its signifying power, including more recent postmodern implications. The potential for objectification and reification present in fragmentation, especially in the fragmentation of the body that Theodor W. Adorno pointed out in the Surrealists and that Georg Lukács condemned as a matter of formal aberration on the part of modernist and avant-garde artists in general, is certainly evoked as one position in *Syntagma*'s grand treatment of fragmentation. When used in

Women's legs on a staircase

conjunction with the concern for movement, the split frames (frequently dividing the images of the woman), the truncated body parts, and the fragmentation implicit in the multimedia approach are at times reminiscent of the frenetic pace and hyper-space of what Jean Baudrillard calls simulation, the reign of the "un-bound" sign. In this realm, which lacks delimitation of any sort, the sky is literally the limit. As Baudrillard explains, centrifugal forces, unhampered by the "work of the negative," through which "all *Aufhebung* [sublation] is experienced [*ressentie*] as *Aufschiebung* [postponement]," result in the annihilation of time "by pure circulation."[7] At other times these fragments in motion grind to a pernicious halt, a state of inertia, which Paul Virilio has so brilliantly analyzed as just the flip side of the violence of speed.

With a slight shift in text and context, however, these same formal strategies become the instruments of reappropriation, of self-directed and self-possessed movement. When fragments are looked at as an opportunity to avoid closed systems, taking structures apart and selecting each part for its value as raw material; when doubling creates a distance that leads to historical insights—the process of reappropriation is well under way. In other words, formal considerations alone do not define what is avant-garde in *Syntagma*. Or maybe it would be more correct to say that they do not define what is avant-garde in a political, feminist sense.

The disappearance of the body, a phenomenon of the 1980s described by Baudrillard and others, is a direct consequence of the place assigned to the body in a system of signs that is based on a "hermeneutics of life as lack, castration, and death."[8] Similarly, the notion of femininity in poststructuralist thought remains a textual, metaphorical construct disregarding real women, their experience, and histories. "The question of woman for the male philosophers is a question of style (of discourse, language, writing—of philosophy),"[9] writes Teresa de Lauretis, in an attempt to guard against the evacuation of politics from feminist discourse through the elimination of its material base: individual, concrete women.

The theoretical possibility of the disappearance of the body is satirically depicted in Export's contribution to the omnibus film *The Seven Deadly Sins* (1987). There she describes "Lust" (the sin of her choice) in terms of the ultimate identification and extension of the body through advertising market strategies. A modern form of prostitution is to turn the living body into a billboard, a practice already well established among successful athletes. In this context, the completely straightforward endorsement of the body as signifier, so crucial to all of Export's previous work, raises important questions. In both cases we are dealing with the identity of body and signifier. The question then revolves around the terms of this identification. Whereas in some postmodern equations the body is subsumed under the signifier, in Export's work the focus is on the body as existential ground of every woman. However stylized a study of the body as signifier *Syntagma* may be, it is about the signifying power of the body, not about the embodiment of the signifier.

At the very least, it would be playing with essentialist fires to claim the body to be the existential ground of every woman, and yet, unless this claim is upheld to some extent, the very notion of materiality becomes meaningless. It was and is important to counter biological determinism with an insistence on the social construction of subjects and subject positions; however, to deny the role played by the individual body altogether, that is, not to theorize individual bodies, results only in social determinism and its attendant denial of agency. The irony of the position that places such high stakes on its materialist approach is that it reverts to a most curious form of idealism that grants reality only to the law. In her effort to rethink the problem of essentialism, Diana Fuss points to this paradoxical reversal when she writes: "To insist that essentialism is always and everywhere reactionary is, for the constructionist, to buy into essentialism in the very act of making the charge; it is to act as if essentialism has an essence."[10] With reference to Irigaray's overt definition of women from an essentialist, body-centered standpoint, Fuss argues that this position also has its political advantage insofar as it represents a form of resistance: "a woman will never be a woman solely in a masculine order" (61). Such a strategic deployment of essentialism then can break through the deadlock an extreme form of antiessentialism has imposed on feminist discourse. This debate could be taken a step further by placing it in the context of revision of the absolute subject–object dichotomy. I would venture to say that the reactionary use of essentialism hinges in the first place on the dualistic opposition of the body to mental processes. If these rigid polarities could give way to a model of dynamic interchange between otherwise abstract essences, questions of historical, cultural, geographic, class, and gender specificity would be emphasized as a matter of course in theoretical analyses. The value of Irigaray's re-metaphorizing the body and her attempt at symbolizing the female imaginary along metonymic lines ultimately lies in proposing a model of logic, the logic of ambiguity, which Fuss has described as an economy of "ceaseless exchange" and "constant flux" summarized in the three words "both at once," or negatively, "neither one nor two" (58).

Export has pitted the expansive body against encroachments of all kinds on the matrix of our being. It is defined by the extent and measure not only of its mobility but also of its signifying power and communicative ability. Although much of her performance work is engaged in exteriorizing internal states (that is, bringing psychic material to expression), signification is not limited to that. The body is also embedded in and part of a system of communication. It is neither identical with this system nor immune to it. Affected by all the factors that go into defining a particular social and cultural environment, it in turn exerts its own influence through psychosomatic peculiarities. Releasing the body into the mobility of signifying interrelations meant, for Export, emphasizing technological media like film and video from the outset for their expansive potential.

In her article "The Real and Its Double: The Body,"11 Export reassesses the expansive body and the nature–technology continuum in terms of its usefulness for women in the 1980s. Departing from Freud's pronouncement in *Civilization and Its Discontents* that technology represents the perfection and expansion of the human body, a telos at the end of which towers a kind of prosthetic god, she compares this animation of a mechanized future to the avenues of development open to women. Because of their absence from the story of civilization, women's recourse is to the natural world, a more ancient animism based, however, on the same principle as that of technology: the infusion of human modes of life into the organic and inorganic environment—that is, fetishism in the anthropological sense. The expansiveness available to women is based on their identification with the biological body, which only reinforces their state of division, difference, and alienation from the course of human civilization. A vicious circle, a black hole: from the bottom of this split and informed by it, Export urges women to abandon the reproductive functions of the body in order to usher in its genuine transformation. She argues for a different kind of expansiveness, one available through mobility and discourse, transportation and communication, technologically enhanced.

How does this proposition differ from the deathblow dealt to the body by our postmodern fathers? Does it not simply follow another prescription for further marginalization of women? Is it not an act of bad faith; in other words, is it not conceding that biology is in fact at the root of women's destiny rather than the act of disempowering them? Export conceives of her theoretical position as both provocative and consistent with her feminist strategies since the 1960s. It is provocative insofar as it is a deliberate act of bad faith to bring to attention the absurdity of a civilization that execrates the very foundation of its continued existence. Perhaps this act of provocation would stimulate women to adopt as the mythological basis of their own psychic and cultural genesis not some construction—however exquisitely forged—parallel to the Oedipal myth, but incipient patriarchy's wishful and fraudulent dream of Athena's birth in full armor from the head of Zeus: a prosthetic goddess, as it were. And perhaps such a straightforward disavowal and desertion of the place of the maternal would carry enough explosive power to change the course of women's history. Far from being suppressed, the body is featured in this feminist action in its performance-refusal, a demonstrative pulling out of vicious circulation. It is another strategic deployment of the body, one that makes its mark through negation.

In the meantime, expansiveness finds new avenues. In a later sequence of *Syntagma*, the woman sits at a table, writing by hand. Behind her as a backdrop are the gigantic pages of a book, which are periodically turned by an invisible hand. The camera slowly pans to the left of this scene and focuses on the screen of the video monitor showing the same table and woman; only here, the woman is using a typewriter. Panning back again to the first writing scene, the camera rests on the woman, who is now using a typewriter as well. These pans are repeated three times in different constellations. In the last set, the silhouette of a bicycle, symbol of emancipated mobility for the suffragettes, can be made out behind the woman's back. Mounted like the rest of *Syntagma* in complex layers of video and film, this passage is not just a historical survey on the importance of technology for the women's movement; it also shifts the film's investigation of the body—in fragments and in motion—into another gear: verbal discourse and communication.

Communication is the one category that allows the seemingly contradictory and disparate approaches to be seen as a series of displacements rather than as oppositions. In Export's work, the body has never represented the source of natural wholeness uncontaminated by culture, or the idyllic retreat into fantasies of bliss. On the contrary, as I have tried to show, it is conceived as thoroughly cultural and endowed with the power to signify. At the same time that the body's materiality is foregrounded, this materiality is conceived as a dynamic field that both effects changes and is being changed. The absence of verbal language in most of Export's experimental work has as much to do with a skepticism toward language inherited from the literary strategies of the fifties (of the *Wiener Gruppe*) as it does with the effort to bridge the subject–object rift between culture and nature, through the recognition that body language is inextricably bound to verbal language, that there are differences in mediation and immediacy, but that there is no radical break between the

Camera mounted on window

two kinds of communication. The inclusion of writing in *Syntagma* is thus not so much a contradiction to earlier work as it is another instance of expansiveness. The revaluation of verbal language and writing in the theory of the eighties no doubt has contributed to this development.

In the search for the bodily existence of women, the avant-garde among women artists today finds itself in a position similar to that of their male predecessors in the 1920s with regard to the realization that new technology can only be ignored at the risk of becoming ineffectual. If the "power is knowledge and knowledge is information" equation is correct for our time, then this is also the condition of women's existence, and women cannot afford to neglect technological developments. *Syntagma* ends on an exquisite note: the woman we have seen throughout the film closes the window in the apartment. But since a camera is mounted on the inside as well as on the outside of the window, inside and outside are simultaneously recorded. Having spent two decades in bridging the gap between inside and outside, subject and object, between the body and signification, Export is taking the steps necessary to avoid renewed polarization stemming from new means and instruments of communication and information. How that information is used is another matter altogether, and it can only be decided once women are not just the stuff that cities are made of, but their architects.

Films for Television

The Armed Eye (Das bewaffnete Auge, 1984)

T*he Armed Eye* is the first of Export's four films written for and commissioned by Austrian television. It is subtitled "Valie Export in a Dialogue with the Film Avant-garde" and consists of three parts, each of which is forty-five minutes long. All three parts are shot in video. The purpose of this miniseries is explicitly didactic and educational. Since Export did not direct the final cutting of the material she had compiled in a script, she does not claim it as her own insofar as the overall composition is concerned, since the discrepancies between her conception and the final execution of the project are substantial. Nevertheless, her selection of materials and the approximate structure of the film presented by her as "host" is worth a brief review.

Each of the three segments begins with a variation of one of Export's own works, namely "Ping Pong," the interactional expanded movie from the late 1960s, used here as both her logo and an invitation to the viewers not to "consume" the following program but to respond to it critically. The first part is entitled "Staged Space–Staged Time" (Inszenierter Raum–Inszenierte Zeit) and focuses on film as medium, on the phenomenon of reproduced movement, of rhythm and dynamics. It consists of a series of visual and verbal quotations taken from artists and scientists who have contributed to the exploration of the problem of movement in space and time and to rendering visible in successive stages and detail what exceeds the human eye. In rough outline, the founders of cinematography—Marey, Gilbreth, and Muybridge—as well as avant-garde artist Marcel Duchamp are followed by more recent contributors to this subject in avant-garde film: Ed Emshwiller, Werner Nekes, Michael Snow, Klaus Wyborny, Heinz Emigholz, Hans Scheugl, Rotraut Pape, and, closer to home, Peter Weibel and Export herself.

Part two, entitled "Montage and Narrative Film" (Montage und Narrativer Film), again departs from the notion of cinema as apparatus that includes the spectator and his/her subjective perception. The ability of film to create an impression of a reality is matched by the audience's readiness to perceive it as such. The possibility of manipulating perception through a succession of synchronic–asynchronic–synchronic image and sound effects is demonstrated in the film *Match Box*, by Polish filmmaker Wojciech Bruszewski. More examples, from films by Marc Adrian and Malcolm Le Grice, support this demonstration. A final example, from *Invisible Adversaries* (the fish and cosmetic preparation passage), introduces a full-fledged debate about montage as the basis of "film language," thanks to which film is more than the mere reproduction of an event. Quotations from Pudowkin, examples from Eisenstein, and a lengthy treatment of Maya Deren's vertical montage with examples from *Meshes of the Afternoon* round out this debate. After a short autobiographical insert, discussion moves to more recent examples of rhythmic and serial sequences and their effect on perception by Kurt Kren, Michael Snow, Gary Beydler, Herwig Kempinger, and Export (*Menschenfrauen*). Excerpts from Moucle Blackout's *Birth of Venus*, Linda Christanell's *Anna*, and Anne Severson's *I change, I am the same* bring this section to a close.

The third and final part, entitled "Structural Film," begins with an excerpt from Richard Serra's *Hand Catching Lead* as visual accompaniment to P. Adams Sitney's definition of structural film in terms of rigid camera, the flicker effect, loops, and the filming of projections. Peter Kubelka, Paul Sharits and Tony Conrad, Stan Brakhage, George Landow, Hollis Frampton, and Peter Gidal are cited as important representatives of this group of avant-garde filmmakers. Differences from Sitney's extreme formalist position are found in Hans Scheugl and Ernst Schmidt, Jr., and their notion of structural films as films that take their principle of construction from the film material itself, or films that are structured by an outside concept. The development of avant-garde films in England is presented as strongly influenced by the theoretical positions of Althusser, of psychoanalysis, and of semiology.

Within this final part is a middle segment dedicated to those avant-garde artists who have attended to the materials and processes of cinematic reproduction themselves. This represents a step further in the direction of formal/material experiments to include not just structural considerations but the possibilities of the film prior to any aesthetic or conceptual ordering. Man Ray's technique in photograms is briefly explained as precursory to a great number of more recent films, some of which—such as Stan Brakhage's *Mothlight,* Wilhelm and Birgit Hein's *Rohfilm,* and Ernst Schmidt's *Wienfilm*—are shown in excerpts to illustrate this connection. William Raban, J. M. Maziere, and Liz Rhodes are also mentioned as representatives of this group of formal/ material experimenters.

A special homage to Austrian avant-garde cinema rounds out the final part of *The Armed Eye.* Its beginning dates back to the early fifties, with films made by Herbert Vesely, Peter Kubelka, Ferry Radax, and Kurt Kren, and independently from this group, Marc Adrian, who lived in Hamburg at that time. The formal aspects of this group were first influenced by Schönberg's and Webern's twelve-tone and serial music. Later, in the sixties, the Austrian Filmmaker's Cooperative was founded by the next generation of film artists, with some overlap of the early group (as in the case of Kurt Kren). The other members were Hans Scheugl, Ernst Schmidt, Jr., Peter Weibel, Gottfried Schlemmer, and Valie Export herself. At the same time, some members of the group of Viennese Actionists (Otto Muehl and Günther Brus, for example), were soon interested in film, on the one hand as a means of documenting their performances and, on the other, to develop actions especially for film. The spreading of experimental super-8 mm films began around the mid-seventies. Although it was an international movement, this section deals with Austria, and thus only three representatives are discussed: Lisl Ponger, Dietmar Brehm, and Gudrun Bielz. *The Armed Eye* closes with Yvonne Rainer's *Film About a Woman Who,* a successful example, it is explained, of how a feature film can accommodate the insights gained by experimental films while at the same time avoiding the dogmatic tendencies inherent in some of these works.

Table Quotes (Tischbemerkungen, 1985)

This forty-five-minute film is composed and directed by Valie Export. It is mainly shot in video (by Export) with a few 8 mm and 16 mm inserts. *Table Quotes* is a study in ambivalence. The title already points in that direction with its connotation of political importance (roundtable talks) juxtaposed to the domestic and casual setting of an ordinary dining table, which functions as anchor to the lofty intellectualism of the film's subject, a portrait of Oswald Wiener. Wiener was born in 1935, and studied law, music, African languages, and mathematics. He was one of the members of the Wiener Gruppe in the fifties, and in 1969 published his main work, *The Improvement of Central Europe: A Novel (Die Verbesserung von Mitteleuropa, Roman).* Export's close friendship with Wiener and especially with his wife, Ingrid, guarantees a fairly straightforward homage to one of the protagonists of the Viennese avant-garde. At the same time her view is necessarily that of a woman who has to work twice as hard to be situated anywhere near the mythic heights of her male predecessors. Yet there is no open criticism; nothing in the information presented points to an overt attack or even aggression.

The ambivalence resides entirely in how Export structures her material and in the camera's point of view.

In the opening sequence some of these strategies become immediately apparent in the intercutting of two video tracks. In one, Wiener shaves, bathes, and brushes his teeth; the other sequence shows him all dressed up, the finished product of these hygienic and thoroughly pedestrian efforts, expounding in profound seriousness on his status as poet and what that status means in terms of his perception of everyday processes and of other people. While the sound track privileges his voice from the finished product track, the visuals are almost entirely taken from the shaving sequence. Extremely detailed close-ups, unusual camera angles, exaggerated low angles (for example, revealing the underside of his sudsy chin) provide not only a comic counterexploration of his physical persona, but also detract from the spoken word. They gain such visual momentum that they compel the viewer's attention away from the deliberate and meandering self-reflection of the speaker. But his words are not always drowned out. Long passages are given over to his thoughts on the nature of perception, on the theory of knowledge, on his relation to cities and to the wilderness (a substantial part of the image track explores his current residence, Dawson City, Canada, and its natural environment); his questions regarding the notion of freedom; or to his pithy definition of nihilism as "that kind of mentality which is convinced from the beginning of the possibility of formalizing and mechanizing all human concerns and which corresponds in practice to a sense of worthlessness and aimlessness." These passages are also intercut or interrupted by everyday trivia, or by his hobbies, which include flying airplanes, playing chess, and playing music.

Another, perhaps far too delicate, undertone of distanciation from the avowed subject surfaces intermittently but sparingly throughout the film. It has to do with the tantalizing oscillation between the absence and presence of his wife Ingrid, the assumed but not acknowledged substratum of his life. Soon after the opening sequence, the camera departs from its object of portraiture and focuses on a painting by the Austrian Maria Lassnig, a portrait of Oswald and Ingrid Wiener in which the wife, in an idealized reversal of the actual relations of power, takes up the foreground of the canvas. Export's videotape is more realistic and derives its effect precisely from calling attention to the marginalization of Ingrid's person. Her off-screen voice, asking whether it is time to eat; a long shot of her carrying cases of beer into the house; and the set table which the husband matter-of-factly sits down to, only to retire to a couch afterwards to continue his ruminations: all are more eloquent testimony of the imbalance that underlies his wise stance. Throughout the passages focusing on Oswald Wiener, the camera stays very close to him as if trying to absorb him in this exercise, perhaps attempting to deconstruct his mythic stance through the persistent focus on the details of his physique and the physiognomy of his intellect.

The Yukon Quest (1986)

In a sense, this forty-five-minute tape, shot in video and 16 mm film, is a continuation of *Table Quotes*. A joint venture conceived by Export and Oswald and Ingrid Wiener as an adventure film, *The Yukon Quest* is based on their interest in the Canadian and Alaskan wilderness, with the added attraction of following the famous Yukon Quest dogsled races from Alaska to Canada. A brief insert of the races already appears as a preview in *Table Quotes*. The distribution of responsibilities in making the film was fairly even. Export was in charge of the overall direction of the film. Ingrid kept a diary that functioned as part of the connective tissue of the film text. Oswald wrote the text passages explaining the historical and geographical background of the race, and in addition, coordinated the shooting. The tape was a great success with Austrian Television and ratings were very high. Another joint project with the Wieners is already planned; it is an exploration of religious sects that purport to speak in tongues. The full title of this new project is: *Speaking in Tongues: To Speak the Un-*

speakable. Glossolalia Among Native Peoples, in Christian Faith,
as Emergency Language and as Poetic Experiment. Production of
this new film for television began in the summer of 1992.

Actionism International (Aktionskunst International, 1989)

This last film for television, seventy-three minutes in length, is
another educational project, very similar in tone and structure to
the first three-part series, *The Armed Eye.* It was originally shot
almost in its entirety on 16 mm film. Export wrote the script and
this time also directed it. She no longer appears personally to
present the material; instead, an invisible professional female
speaker reads the commentary text that accompanies a montage of visual and verbal quotations. The verbal quotations are
frequently presented in the form of statements by the respective
artists or theoreticians themselves.

The tape gives an overview of the neo–avant-garde after 1945,
and in addition supplies an analytic-theoretical background to
its various configurations. While the style of the new avant-garde
is acknowledged to be international, the film nevertheless tries
to do justice to national specifics. Thus, the first movement
discussed is the Wiener Gruppe, constituted between 1952
and 1955 by Gerhard Rühm, Konrad Bayer, H. C. Artmann,
Friedrich Achleitner, and Oswald Wiener. Their "First Literary
Cabaret" in 1958 was also called a *Begebenheit,* German for
"happening." In their opening act, the entire ensemble sat on
rows of chairs facing the audience as Wiener explained that the
situation was now reversed, that the audience were the actors,
while the group on stage considered themselves the audience.
One of the splinter groups of the Wiener Gruppe, the so-called
"Hundsgruppe" (dog group), was already involved in the early
fifties in very Happening-like actions, such as the destruction of
a piano with an axe or their "concerto grosso," featuring several
people walking and jumping on the keys of a piano.

Careful attention is given to the Situationist International in
Paris, which Export considers the "strongest verbal form" in

Europe to break through toward a new concept of art. In Export's view, Guy Debord, the Situationists' main theorist, anticipates contemporary concepts of simulation and hyperreality that have catapulted their propagators Marshall McLuhan and Jean Baudrillard into influential positions in art circles in the eighties. Debord's pessimist analysis of the classical avant-gardes resulted in his negative assessment of visual images, which in a "society of spectacles" are reduced to the status of commodities. In keeping with his Marxist roots, Debord saw the only possible solution to the problem of cultural creation in a new advance of world revolution. A statement by Baudrillard clarifies the difference between his position and that of the Situationists with whom he was not directly involved, but whose antimedia strategies have fascinated him since the early sixties. The difference, as he sees it, lies in the Situationists' key notion of spectacle as a form of alienation. His own concept of simulation has done away with the whole mechanism of spectacle, its scenes, actors, and dramaturgy. Simulation is the hallmark of a totally integrated society, in which the possibility (of which the Situationists dreamt) to subvert the codes of art, media, and philosophy is no longer given. Baudrillard describes the paradox implicit in the transition from the Situationists of twenty years ago to today's simulationists as follows: "While the Situationists searched out strong, intense situations, the Simulationists continuously repeat art, they develop by searching for a kind of strategy for simulated images. Here an attempt is made to find a strategy for simulation without first finding a strategy of the situation. Is there such a thing as a strategy of simulation?" A brief discussion of related groups such as Cobra (a group of painters: Carl Henning, Pedersen, Pierre Alchinsky, Constant, Corneille, Karel Appel), Spur (a Munich-based group: Zimmer, Sturm, Prem, Fischer), and Kommune 1 in Berlin, along with statements by Jorgen Nash and Jens Jorgen Thorsen, brings this section to a close.

The development of the neo–avant-garde in the United States is traced from its inception at Black Mountain College and John

Cage's *Theater Piece Nr. 1* in 1952, generally known as the first Happening, through Fluxus, Inter-media, and Performance art. A statement by Allan Kaprow pinpoints a number of important steps in this development, such as the transition from action painting to Actions and Happenings themselves, or the move to replace objects with the human body. Fluxus, which succeeded Happenings, is presented predominantly as a movement in music, with a strong influence on Minimal Music, Concept Art, Land Art, and Inter-media Art. The difference between mixed-media and Inter-media is explained in a statement by Dick Higgins: "In Inter-media the different media are conceptually fused, you cannot distinguish them. With multi-media or mixed-media they are easily distinguished, although they are happening simultaneously."

In France, Happenings developed out of the object art of the group of *Nouveaux Realists* such as Yves Klein and Arman. In contrast to the American Happening artists, the performances and Happenings of Wolf Vostell, Josef Beuys, and Tomas Schmit in Germany are characterized as "more political." Similarly, the impulse behind the movement of Viennese Actionists Brus, Muehl, Nitsch, and Schwarzkogler is located in their desire to break the state's monopoly on representing reality, whereby their preferred procedure is that of transgressing against socially agreed-upon taboos. In this context, Export explains her own concept of Feminist Actionism as the "attempt to dissociate the self of woman from the body." The women, whose names are at least mentioned, but whose work and statements are in most cases presented in this tape, include Carolee Schneemann, Yoko Ono, Lynn Hershman, Ulrike Rosenbach, Karen Finley, Cindy Sherman, Gina Pane, Charlotte Moorman, Marina Abramovic, and Laurie Anderson.

Finally, performance artist Vito Acconci thematizes the difference between performances and actions:

> the classical "Action" is, in principle, less tied to the performer and
> more to the body. Important are materials, objects, the audience, real

space and time . . . "Performance" has emphasized the body and the media simultaneously in the quality of mis-en-scène and in the person of the performer. The cultural, medial coding of the body and the person and not of the body as material, are central.

This emphasis on the person characterizes the Performance Art of the seventies. In the eighties, multimedia performances, often based in music, are the heirs to the Action Art forms of the previous decades. The tape ends with a statement by Mark Pauline about "junk sculptures" and the change in what is considered junk over the last thirty years, accompanied by the fascinating performances of his Survival Research Laboratories in San Francisco and New York.

A Perfect Pair (Ein perfektes Paar, 1986)

This twelve-minute contribution in 16 mm to the omnibus film *Seven Women–Seven Sins* (Sieben Frauen–Sieben Sünden) produced by German Television (ZDF) is an allegorical reflection on the modern meaning of voluptuousness or lust, in its ancient sense of moral transgression and capital sin, whereby allegory is finally absorbed by satire in the sinister twist on the notion of sin and morality. The connection between morality and power is established immediately in one of the first scenes: A young woman, dressed in white with a wreath in her hair and an Easter lily, symbol of purity, in her hand, distributes the host of holy communion to the passersby. Her breasts are bare and encased in a little portable glass shrine, like the relics of the saints. The hosts she hands out are imprinted with the logos of different business firms, as if to spread the news that the administration of chastity has changed proprietors.

Meanwhile, Nelly, the old-fashioned whore of Babylon, seated on a bar stool selling her flesh inch by inch to the winners in a lottery of sexual favors, is instructed that with a little updating, her sinful trade of yore could be converted into a modern virtue. Instead of selling her skin, all she would have to do is to think of herself as billboard, as an advertisement space for the business powers that be, becoming one of so many extras in their god-like scenarios. The only sin in this vision is one of omission, of not having sold oneself, which the chorus of social misfits, sitting under a table, confesses to be ashamed of. Nelly's angel of enlightenment and salvation—a bodybuilder—demonstrates these new virtues, decorated as he is all over his body with the logos of various companies. Their marriage is finally con-sum(at)ed in the ritual exchange of bizarre articles of clothing, each of which is designed to promote a different product. In this dystopic fantasy, the ordinary body in the street can earn his/her living by spraying logos on any of its parts with the aid of vending machines in reverse. It is the ultimate El Dorado of salesmanship, in which the human body is no longer just objec-tified but has literally merged with signs.

A Perfect Pair is Export's only comedy to date. Much of the muffled humor in her earlier work has finally found a full-fledged if brief outlet in this short piece. From the zany concep-tion to the phantasmagoric costumes, startling computer graphics, dense symbolism, and brisk pacing, it is a sparkling satire without the biting ill humor that attaches to much of this genre. In its own way it is also a continuation of her past concern with the body as bearer of social codes. This notion is here in its literal application taken ad absurdum. At the same time, its comical implications are never devoid of serious critique of the marketing strategies to which the human body increasingly falls subject. The dialogic use of music, also unique to this film, adds to the critical humor. In the introductory sequence, the body-builder works out to Marilyn Monroe's song "He Doesn't Look Like Much of a Lover" and later to "I'm Just a Simple Man"; church music accompanies Nelly's dressing up in her wedding gown, which is covered with pornographic images, and then blends into the tango "I Have Forgotten Your Name, but I'll Never Forget Your Kisses." The objectification of woman in prostitution is extended here to the institution of marriage. And beyond that, *A Perfect Pair* points toward the status of the human body, regardless of gender, as free-floating, disposable, and interchangeable sign in a totally integrated society, in which the dimension of critical evaluation is absent.

Interview with Valie Export

ROSWITHA MUELLER: Since the beginning of your engagement in the arts in the mid-sixties, you have been interested in the technological media and you have especially concerned yourself with the potentials of the new electronic and digital processes. What has sustained this experimental attitude over the years?

VALIE EXPORT: The technological media allow for a new kind of image production, which is completely different from earlier image productions such as painting. I am mainly interested in the difference in materials as the condition for artistic statement. The image production in digital technology is based on the construction of models. In this case I see image production also as the production of models, which allows me to expand and continually change the process of representation, which has been important for my entire artistic production. A few years ago I began work with the computer. I confronted analogic photography with digital photography, in order to foreground the disjunction between the two media. Then I transferred the digital photography to different materials, for example, textiles, transparent materials, chemical materials, etc. I can also use digital images for holograms or for cyberspace. It is always my goal *not* to create a photo-realistic environment, which is how it is mostly used at this point.

RM: I am very interested in this notion of models. What puzzles me is that it seems to be such a static and normative approach, when all your efforts are directed toward change.

VE: Certainly, it is true that models are static which can be a disadvantage for the artistic process since they evoke uniformity. In contrast, in painting, the gestures of the hand, body, and mind can be expressed freely. But in the nonobjective art of the classical avant-garde, signs of a model character can already be detected. Digital technology determines our view of the world today and in turn this technology was informed by our mathematical explanation of the universe. The question is whether this is the only representation of our world. I don't think so.

RM: Since your stated goal is *not* to create photo-realism, do you search for specific strategies, depending on the particular medium you are using, to counteract its effect of realism?

VE: Every medium has its own relation to what we call reality and can be subverted in its own specific way to counteract this effect. What is most important to me is to have at my disposal different languages of expression and of meaning. I define language here in the broader sense as a system of signs and meanings. Society restricts the plurality and differences of languages by demanding that only one language be used—its language, the language of socially sanctioned ideology—while discriminating against and exiling divergent elements. My works may be following philosophical, social, cultural, sexual, psychological, or technological insights; and for each of these avenues the medium of expression and of artistic representation is different and can also pursue various methods. In other words, not only the means of expression but the themes are important to me, since I am interested in showing aspects of the phenomenal world. Multidimensionality, transformation, and difference are the common denominators of my work. I sometimes have termed my productions "medial anagrams."

RM: Can you describe how medial anagrams function in your work?

VE: Medial anagrams are units of representation which are transposed into different contexts and codifications. What interests me is that even minimal shifts in context will bring out differences in signification for the same unit of representation. It is a kind of language system for image production in the technological media.

RM: This technique has been likened to postmodern strategies of the deconstruction of identity and to a fascination with simulation. Does this correspond to your intent?

VE: I am interested in postmodern theories of the subversion of the subject since I would like to dissolve the traditional view of the subject, which had contributed to the oppression of women. It could also be helpful in freeing women from social norms and enforced codes like motherhood. But I do not follow the postmodern philosophers when they equate the question concerning women's subjectivity with a confirmation of phallocentrism. The phenomenological attempt to overcome Hegel's dialectics in certain postmodern theories seems rather conservative to me.

RM: An Austrian male critic took it upon himself to characterize the mode of production specific to women as "polytechnical dilettantism." How do you respond to this term and do you think we still need to be concerned about defining a feminist aesthetics?

VE: The term "polytechnical" is justified. This mode of production has its base in the position of women as "other" both in the world of art and in society. It is a consequence of the necessity to inscribe my text into the text of the "other" in order to make it acceptable and to communicate in the first place. But the label "dilettantism" is not appropriate. It derives from the difference in the system of values and norms established by men, which is a type of colonizing view similar to the way Europe as a whole looks at the cultures of so-called savages. The "dilettantism" of male artists, on the contrary, was enthusiastically affirmed by Modernism and Neo-Expressionism.

I work in different media because I cannot confine myself to one single one, since each medium adds a different dimension to my work. I do claim professional status for my work but not in the manner of the art market, which is for me capitalist professionalism, design, and overproduction. The *documenta 8* where everything was raised to a gigantic level demonstrated that very well. In our society things exist only in their commodity form, including ideology. That is the double dilemma for women. How should a work of art look if it must confirm the commodity woman and the commodity art? The work of some women artists *follows* aesthetic concepts that are informed by phallic structures. More often than not, these attempts are marked by immediate success.

RM: This argument would seem to support the specificity of feminist aesthetics, not just as a consequence of women's marginality to the art market but structurally as well.

VE: There definitely are structures specific to women, but they are not inherent, eternal forms; they are time-bound results of our feminist debates and feminine acculturation. I agree with Irigaray's so-called "essentialist" intervention, which to me is not so much essentialist as it is a counterstrategy at a specific historical point in time to the determination of women's bodies by male tradition.

RM: In the seventies, video technology was sometimes called a "feminine" medium. You yourself have connected video with feminism. Can you clarify this further?

VE: There is nothing feminine about video and there is nothing masculine about computer technology. Neither is art feminine or masculine. The points of departure of expression, content, and representations may be gender specific but not the medium itself.

If there is male dominance it also means that women have not tried hard enough to get ahold of the media and to use it for their goals. This is hard work because women have never been granted access without a struggle. Yet, it is necessary for us to succeed in this.

On the other hand, we know that video was very important for women artists in the seventies, because the medium was not yet historically coded as male among artists, nor was it hierarchically determined. At the same time, it could provide information about forms of representation which are of great significance in feminist discourse. Video allowed for new explorations of concepts like "truth," "nature," and "reality." New technologies shed new light on problems involving notions of the imaginary, the fictional, and the real.

RM: To take a concrete example, can you imagine that your video *Silent Language* could be as effectively produced in any medium other than video?

VE: It could be done in cyberspace, but the meaning of representation is totally different. Cyberspace uses imaginary bodies, which means that the interesting clash between the fictional bodies of the ancient painting and the living body of the modern woman will disappear, because the body of the modern woman will naturally be based on the model of the frozen image from history. In that sense the whole point would be lost. In other words, history cannot be represented in cyberspace in this way, because this break on the level of representation is no longer visible.

RM: How does your contention that the new media expand our description and perception of the world apply to digital technology, since that technology no longer directly reproduces images from external reality.

VE: In the analogic media like film and photography or video, the image comes from the outside into the apparatus. There is an external reality, which, in whatever way, is reproduced. For some years now I have confronted digital photography with analogic photography, the images from the outside with the images from the inside.

RM: When you say "images from the inside," you are primarily talking about images that are technically produced inside the apparatus. Do you think that this is the continuation, by means of technology, of what the classical avant-garde has tried to achieve in the first place—to distance itself and break with the reproduction of reality?

VE: Naturally, it is a continuation of one of the aims of the avant-garde, to part with the reproduction of reality. But it is more complex than that. In other movements of the more recent avant-gardes, one has tried to bring reality back into art. What I consider important in all of this is the continued investigation and questioning of reality and its reproduction. Interrogating the perception, the concept, and the representation of reality is the crux of all of my work. And the new technologies allow further extensions of this investigation. Human history is the history of representation. As long as we are caught in the dualism of the real and its representation, our thinking will be reduced to binary oppositions, like nature and artefact, or body and mind. I would welcome a departure from this deadlock position.

RM: When you look at the actual uses of digital technology, it seems to me that the opposite is happening. The technology is placed into the service of the simulation of reality. Would that not constitute the epitome of binary reductionism?

VE: Absolutely, and furthermore, here the representation of reality becomes the commodity of reality, "*die wahre Ware*" (the true commodity). The most important potential of digital technology for artists to explore is to invent models of reality and to exercise our power of alternative thinking.

RM: Does this imply a utopian project?

VE: I am not a utopian thinker in the traditional sense, but models of reality can only be utopian constructions. I should add that I am interested not only in the artistic values but also in the imaging of differences and in the inclusion of marginal social forms and interactions.

RM: Is it possible to claim that your work with the body is exactly this mean and mediation between the artistic experiment and the social investigation. That the body is for you on the one hand material for artistic expression and on the other the bearer of social signification?

VE: I have, from the very beginning, considered the human body, in particular the body of woman, as medium in my artistic work. Society in all of its ramifications expresses itself through the body. The body is the principle sign that allows the power of history and history as construction to be experienced and to become visible and therefore changeable. The nexus (Verknüpfung) between body, technological science, and society is a cultural expression of our times that my artistic work and my theoretical investigations attempt to define. The body as bearer of signs demonstrates a common language, which, however, can also render it exchangeable, replaceable, and determinable. Therefore it is of the essence to escape from this codification.

RM: If you advocate the escape from the codification of the body in order to avoid its total social determination, do you have in mind another state for the body to be in, however marginal it may be?

VE: The only way to escape from social or cultural codification is to negate, change, or destroy it. If you negate it you have to live outside of society or dissolve the body and the self, which is no answer. In my view one has to constantly question and change codes and the institutionalization of codes. Some of my deconstructive efforts were aimed in this direction, but it is my experience that one remains caught in the textual system, still dominated by signs. Somehow I sense that there must be a more radical position, but I don't know exactly what it would be.

RM: If you had to search among the many strategies, formal and otherwise, of your work to find an answer to this question, where would you be inclined to look?

VE: All the strategies that aim at the dissolution of the identity of the signs. It would be in my tenacious insistence on difference, on contradictions, multidimensionality, and multilayered, sculptural codification, material and immaterial and ontological differences in the cultural and social process on the one hand, and the transformations of contexts on the other. What is important to me in all this is the use of different languages, such as body language or sign language. I reflect what the appropriate "language" would be for what I want to express. I am also interested in investigating the border regions of different forms (*Formensprachen*) and connecting the space of perception (*Wahrnehmungsraum*) with real space (*Realraum*). These different media- and sign languages constitute the discourse I am concerned with in my work.

RM: How do these strategies relate to what I have called the "expansive body," which I described in the *Syntagma* chapter of this book as your method of reappropriating the body especially for women?

VE: These strategies are the strategies of the "expanded body." There are two kinds of strategies of expression, those that are located in the medium itself and those that have to do with how the medium is implemented. In the first case, for example, choosing video over painting can contribute to a certain liberation because, as I said before, the medium was not yet hierarchically determined in the history of art, and the second point comprises the strategies I have enumerated above. The dialog between technology and body leads to expansive intermedial art forms in the sixties.

RM: This decade is also the period of your most intensive production of Expanded Cinema.

VE: The concept and the intention of my early work in Expanded Cinema was to decode reality as it was manipulated in film, to transport the cinematographic apparatus into the installation of time and space in order to break out of the two-dimensionality of the flat surface. The deconstruction of dominant reality, the deconstruction and abstraction of materials, the attempt to find new forms of communication and to realize them were also in the center of my analysis. My work was concentrated on breaking with the traditional form of cinema, the commercial-conventional sequence of film production, shooting, montage, projection, and to replace them in part with aspects of reality, as new signs of the real. Presentation, product, production, reality form a unity in Expanded Cinema. In the intermedial action *cutting* (1967–68) I did not cut the celluloid but the body-screen illuminated by the lamp of the projector. The sound of cutting [shaving], of breathing, and of the projector without film was the sound track. Lighting, development, and image were simultaneously created in the same instant. Today's Expanded Cinema is the digital, electronic cinema, the simulation of space and time, the simulation of reality, virtual reality, if indeed the concept is realized: not to represent the real but to question it. This concept also applies to cyberspace. In this sense some video installations and techno-body performances of the seventies are the precursors of the cyberspace of the eighties and nineties. The point was to open up limited patterns of perception and representation, limited views of the natural and artificial image and space, and a limited concept of truth and reality. Expanded Cinema found its continuation in my medial body-material performances, into which I introduced the body as sign and code for a social and aesthetic expression.

RM: Along the same lines, the goals of Expanded Cinema as you describe it, with reference to " cutting," of mixing body experiences with elements of the technological process in the present moment or "instant time," could also be considered a precursor of virtual reality, which aims at a conjunction of body and machine and of the body's experience in actual time.

VE: Potentially the goals of Expanded Cinema, body actions, and performances and installations could be continued and taken to another level in cyberspace. In cyberspace the spectator enters into the image space, that is, the spectator becomes the actor, as was attempted in interactive experiments and also in Happenings and Fluxus events. The difference in cyberspace is that everything is on an augmented technological level. The spectator determines the process by his/her reactions, but these reactions can be just a movement of the eye to arrange or rearrange a whole event. One of my next interactive installation pieces will be a confrontation between two eyes: a video camera reflects my eye, but I am looking back, and by a movement of my eye in a certain direction and in conjunction with the computer program, I can destroy the video eye or redesign it.

RM: This marginalization of the body immediately conjures up the postmodern obsolete body, in my mind. Isn't there also an aspect of cyberspace and virtual reality that is completely contrary to your expanded body, an implosion of the body instead of an expansion?

VE: Because of the changeability and the phantasmatic construction of the image as sign, the meaning and the identity of the sign also dissolves. In as far as the human being is a sign, a symbol, an image, the assigned meaning of the individual, which is ideologically constructed, also dissolved because of this extended notion of the image. The body in cyberspace has no referent; everything in cyberspace is a free-floating sign without necessary meaning, which also dissolves the meaning of the body. This arbitrary designation of the sign has been exemplified long before, throughout the whole history of the female body.

But this is precisely the reason why I do not believe in the disappearance of the body, because it is also the site of our feelings, senses, and sensuality. My secret hope is that hidden and unknown horizons will be laid bare. It is true that cyberspace is an artificial space of perception, but the spectator communicates and acts as in reality, that is to say, s/he remains a subject. Maybe the system of cyberspace will succeed in creating dreams that free us from historical traces.

RM: Your planned project about the eyes confronting and destroying each other illustrates not just the noxious quality of the gaze as Sartre had described it; since it is your own eye, the phantom of self-destruction through minimal efforts, like pushing a button, is thematized. In other words, the whole technology debate is opened up in this experiment. It seems to me that the classical avant-garde's enthusiasm for technology is the most in need of revision.

VE: I agree. The classical avant-garde connected their technological enthusiasm either with fascist war or with socialist revolution based on the Enlightenment heritage of progress, and a belief in the ever receding barrier of nature, which the Frankfurt School had critiqued early on as an attitude of domination. This enthusiasm was almost a cult comparable to that of humanism. Now we have to ask ourselves how far nature can be destroyed and with it the basis of survival for an expanding population. Nature can no longer serve culture as it has so far for our societies. A subversive use of technology would be to break with these traditions and modes of production. Maybe it will be precisely the new technologies that will allow us to live in a re-determined social and physical reality. In any case, the delineation of the concept of "nature" is also drawn into question, and technology emerges exactly at the cutting edge between human and animal. Technology is usually pioneered by the military industrial complex. For cyberspace as well, very few of the programs were designed by artists. The challenge for artists now, and especially for women artists, is to take charge and responsibility also for the programs.

RM: The technology of reproduction has figured prominently in some of your writings, especially in "The Body and Its Double." Some women see a danger in your insistence on refusing the biological body's reproduction, seeing in it just another overevaluation of the biological functions of women. In a sense it is the obverse of the equally biologistic notion that the directness of the body's expressions is somehow more "true" or more "real" than words.

VE: First, I do understand the dangers of my recommendation to women to refuse natural reproduction. Yet, I think the whole essentialism debate has to be taken out of its abstract philosophical framework, because there one can always find yet another logical trip-up. What I am trying to call attention to is the necessity to change the whole concept of motherhood, the ideological coercion of women to become mothers and wives that is at the core of the cultural determination of our bodies. Only in this framework can what I say make any sense. Certainly, I do not propose in actuality that an individual woman should no longer give birth if she feels like it; rather, it is the coercion I am trying to counteract. And from this perspective, artificial reproduction is equally dangerous, because it can potentially increase the pressure on women if they are not in charge of their lives and if they are not involved in these debates.

RM: In your engagement with the avant-garde in technology, art, and thought you have arrived at conclusions similar to those of some postmodern theorists who have applied their knowledge of the technological media to cultural and social criticism, yet I come away with a greater sense of hope in your texts, as if the future were not necessarily headed for implosion.

VE: That is because I look at life as an endlessly moving sculpture, an extension of the body's cavity into the galactic labyrinth.

It is a genetic sculpture, billions of years old, and is unfinished. The trope of this sculpture is caught in the realm between reality and potentiality.

Milwaukee, April 1992

NOTES

Introduction

1. Jon Hendricks, *Fluxus Codex* (Detroit: The Gilbert and Lila Silverman Fluxus Collection, 1988), p. 21.
2. Mary Emma Harris, *The Arts at Black Mountain College,* (Cambridge: MIT Press, 1987), p. 245.
3. Harold Rosenberg, *The Anxious Object: Art Today and Its Audience* (Chicago: U of Chicago P, 1966), p. 62.
4. George Maciunas, "Neo-Dada in the United States," trans. Peter Herbo, in *Fluxus Codex,* p. 23.
5. Ibid., p. 21.
6. Oswald Wiener, Preface to *Hermann Nitsch, Orgies Mysteries Theatre* (Darmstadt: Marz Verlag, 1969), p. 21.
7. Ibid.
8. Ibid.
9. Henry Geldzahler, "Happenings: Theater by Painters," in *The New American Cinema,* Gregory Battcock, ed. (New York: Dutton, 1967).
10. Weibel/Export, *Wien-Bildkompendium Wiener Aktionismus und Film* (Frankfurt: Kohlkunstverlag, 1970), p. 307. Unless otherwise stated all translations are my own.
11. Ibid.
12. Peter Gorsen, "The Realization of the Murder of Passion or Hermann Nitsch's Contribution to the Drama of the 'Non-aesthetic,' " in *Hermann Nitsch, Orgies Mysteries Theatre,* p. 33.

1. Expanded Cinema

1. Regina Cornwell, "Some formalist tendencies in the current American avant-garde film," in *Studio International* Vol. 184, No. 948 (Oct. 1972), p. 111.
2. Jurgen Claus, *Expansion der Kunst* (Reinbek/Hamburg: Rowohlt, 1970), pp. 15–16.
3. Stephen Dwoskin, *Film is . . .* (London: Owen, 1975), p. 240.
4. Gene Youngblood, *Expanded Cinema* (London: Studio Vista, 1970), p. 41.
5. Birgit Hein, "Expanded Cinema," In *Film als Film,* Birgit Hein and Wulf Herzogenrath, eds. (Köln: Kölnischer Kunstverein, 1978), p. 254. In her understanding of "structural film," Birgit Hein is close to what Regina Cornwell has described as "a cinema of exploration and analysis, often a didactic one commenting on earlier work and on

other genres of film" (90). Cornwell proposes the term "structuralist film" in order to counter P. Adams Sitney's definition of structural film, which she sees placed by him in uneasy vicinity to a "romantic and symbolist sensibility" (86). She also considers Sitney's treatment of the New American Cinema to be an attempt at "the construction of a grand myth about the unity of the American avant-garde film" (87). (Regina Cornwell, "Structural Film: Ten Years Later," in *The Drama Review*, Vol. 23, No. 3 [September 1979], pp. 77–92).

6. Valie Export, "Expanded Cinema as Expanded Reality," *JAM*, Vol. 1, 4 (July 1991), p. 7.

7. Valie Export, Export Archive.

8. In his article "Happenings: Theater by Painters," Henry Geldzahler makes the following distinction between Happenings and Environments: "The Environment is static in the tradition of the work of art, it is there and can be contemplated, experienced and walked away from like a work of art. A Happening, on the other hand, exists in time as well as in space, and is therefore in composition related rather more to music and to theater than to painting and sculpture" (80). This definition, I believe, is also valid for the environments of Expanded Cinema.

9. A similar project is the 1968 unrealized film project *333,* descriptively subtitled "triple projection." Three rotating projectors would show three independent films adjusted so that their joint projection creates a whole new meaning and context. (Because of the difficulties of installation, the films, which do exist, have never been shown in the required way.) Thus three separate films about a man, a woman, and a child turn into one film about a family. The gender and age divisions highlighted and institutionalized through the traditional family structure are put into question by multiple superimpositions of the various family members. Blotting out the individual features of the family is a signal of the dissolution of the hierarchical structure. The same exercise could be done, as Export has pointed out, for parts of the body, the face, or the universe.

10. Valie Export, Export Archive.

11. Cited by Export in "Expanded Cinema as Expanded Reality."

12. Valie Export, Export Archive.

13. Malcolm Le Grice, *Abstract Film and Beyond* (London: Studio Vista, 1977), p. 123. Le Grice mistakenly assigns *Das magische Auge* only to Peter Weibel, the piece was conceived and executed by both Weibel and Export.

14. Valie Export, Export Archive. Another type of audience intervention, this time on a verbal level, happened in *Ein Familienfilm* (A Family Film, 1968), in which a twenty-minute section of a home movie related to the title of the experiment was commented on and joked about by two actors/participants (Export and Weibel) from the audience. In both *Auf+Ab+An+Zu* and *Ein Familienfilm,* of course, the audience still exists separately from the event, and in this sense these expanded movies only demonstrate the structural possibilities of film rather than actually provide new situations themselves.

15. Ibid.

16. Ibid.

17. Ibid.

2. Performances—Actions—Video—Installations

1. Bruce Barber's early attempt at classification in "Indexing: Conditionalism and Its Heretical Equivalents," in *Performance by Artists,* A. A. Bronson and Peggy Gale, eds. (Toronto: Art Metropole, 1979), pp. 183–204, shows just how difficult such a task can be.
2. Dick Higgins, "Postmodern Performance: Some Criteria and Common Points," in *Performance by Artists,* p. 176.
3. Ibid., p. 179.
4. Ibid.
5. Roland Barthes, "The Death of the Author," in *Image/Music/Text,* trans. Stephen Heath (New York: Hill and Wang, 1977), p. 142.
6. Ibid.
7. Ibid., p. 144.
8. Gislind Nabakowski, "The Flirtation With the 'It,' " in *Performance by Artists,* p. 251.
9. "Feminist Actionism" is a term Valie Export coined in an effort to distinguish her work from Viennese Actionism in general.
10. Valie Export, "Aspects of Feminist Actionism," in *New German Critique* 47 (Spring–Summer 1989), p. 71. It might be worth noting in this context of subject–object unity that in his further elaboration of "writing," Barthes points to what linguists call a "performative" and describes it as "a rare verbal form (exclusively given in the first person and in the present tense) in which the enunciation has no other content (contains no other proposition) than the act by which it is uttered" (*Image/Music/Text,* pp. 145–146).
11. Ibid.
12. Ibid., p. 73.
13. Valie Export, "Expanded Cinema as Expanded Reality," in *JAM,* Vol. 1, no. 4 (July 1991), p. 7.
14. Valie Export, Export Archive.
15. Ibid.
16. Ibid.
17. Anita Prammer, *Valie Export* (Wien: Frauenverlag, 1988), p. 123.
18. Valie Export, Export Archive.
19. Two other actions from the same time period are related to *Homometer I* both in their strong symbolism as well as the inspiration taken from Land Art. *Blutwärme* (Blood Heat, 1973) involves two parallel, shallow ditches running from the beach to the ocean. They are lined with foil, and one is filled with blood. The other is filled with gasoline, which is ignited. Some speculations about the mixing of the various materials are suggested in the sparse text: "Vereinigung = Leben" (unity = life). The other action, *Metallene Gesten* (Metal Gestures, 1973), is a grim reflection on captivity and isolation. The performer lies down, unprotected, curled into a fetal position on a field of ice and snow and surrounded by barbed wire. A furrow filled with burning gasoline is traced in the snow, encircling the entire scene.
20. Jean-François Lyotard, "The Unconscious as Mise-en-scène," in *Performance in Postmodern Culture,* Michel Benamou, ed. (Milwaukee: Center for Twentieth Century Studies, 1977), p. 89.
21. Ibid., p. 94.

22. Ibid., p. 95.
23. Ibid., p. 97.
24. Valie Export, Interview with Andrea Juno, in *Angry Women* (San Francisco: Re/Search Publications, 1991), p. 187.
25. Valie Export, Export Archive.
26. Valie Export, *Austria, Biennale di Venezia* (Vienna: Bundesministerium für Unterricht und Kunst, 1980), p. 84.
27. Ibid., with minor corrections of my own in translation.
28. Valie Export, *Das Reale und sein Double: Der Körper* (Bern: Benteli Verlag, 1987), p. 41.
29. Valie Export, *Valie Export, Works from 1968–1975,* published on the occasion of the participation in the Biennale de Paris, 1975.

   Two other video interactions/performances are closely related to the two parts of *Movement Imagination. Brechbare Regeln meiner Kraft. Ein poetischer Flugversuch* (Breakable Rules of My Strength: A Poetic Attempt to Fly, 1975), performed in Copenhagen, is clearly an offshoot of *Movement Imaginations* and its testing of physical strength. Here the performer is tied up completely with string and placed on a platform. Next to her a bird is also tied with string and attached to a nail in the board. The performer takes the nail out of the board with her teeth in order to free the bird. *Implementation* (1974–75), on the other hand, is derived from *Movement Imagination No. 5*. It also makes use of a bird as part of its material. A projection screen is divided into twenty segments of the same size, consecutively numbered from one to twenty. A bird is attached in the center of the screen with a cord, illuminated by a projector. The bird sits on a stick in front of the screen. Each sector of the screen will be successively scanned by the camera and transmitted to the monitor. Occasionally the bird flies around and can be seen on the monitor if it happens to fly through the square just being scanned.
30. Valie Export, Export Archive.
31. For an excellent account of the significance of Export's interactive work, see Regina Cornwell, "Interactive Art: Touching the Body in the Mind," in *Discourse* 14, 2 (Spring 1992), pp. 203–221.
32. Valie Export, Export Archive.
33. Variations on *Adjungierte Dislokationen II* exist in the form of a draft with the intriguing title "Video–Space–Spiral/Space–Video–Drawing." In this version, a black rope is used to form a spiral whose outer circumference is as wide as the room, and is attached to the walls at about the same height as the frontal camera of the performer. It comes to an end (the narrow part of the spiral) at the height of the dorsal camera. By pacing the spiral walk, the performer draws the room, which is recorded on one monitor on a horizontally split screen.

3. Photography

1. Floris M. Neususs, ed., *Photography as Art/Art as Photography 2* (Kassel: Gesamthochschule Kassel, 1977), p. 3.
2. Susan Sontag, *On Photography* (New York: Penguin Books, 1973), p. 140.
3. Pierre Bourdieu, *Eine illegitime Kunst* (Frankfurt: Suhrkamp, 1983) p. 89.

4. Christian Metz, "Photography and Fetish," in *The Critical Image,* Carol Squiers, ed. (Seattle: Bay Press, 1990), p. 156.

5. Floris M. Neususs and Renate Heyne, "Photography in the Art of the 'Seventies," in *Photography as Art—Art as Photography* (Cologne: DuMont, 1979), p. 23.

6. Valie Export, expressed in conversation.

7. Valie Export, *Austria, Biennale di Venezia* (Vienna: Bundesministerium für Unterricht und Kunst, 1980), p. 88.

8. Ibid., p. 92.

9. Margarethe Jochimsen, "Photo-Texts: Confusing Interplay," in *Photography as Art—Art as Photography,* p. 135.

10. Valie Export, *Photography as Art—Art as Photography,* p. 61.

11. A large selection of photos from *Body Configurations in Architecture* as well as from these following series has been published in *Körpersplitter* (Linz: Edition Neue Texte, 1980), ed. Heimrad Bäcker.

12. Valie Export, "Corpus More Geometrico," *ConText* (Vienna: Secession, 1987), p. 20.

13. Rosalind E. Krauss, *The Originality of the Avant-Garde and Other Modernist Myths* (Cambridge: MIT Press, 1985), p. 109.

14. Walter Benjamin, "Kleine Geschichte der Photographie," in *Gesammelte Schriften,* Vol. 2 (Frankfurt: Suhrkamp, 1977), p. 379.

4. *Invisible Adversaries*

1. Claude Lévi-Strauss, *The Savage Mind* (Chicago: University of Chicago Press, 1966), p. 19.

2. In her article "Helke Sander and the Will to Change," in *Discourse 6* (Fall 1983), Kaja Silverman notes "an intense resistance in Sander's work to boundaries both of a formal and discursive kind" (10). This notion of border crossing is extremely useful for feminism and for feminist artists like Export in particular, since it brings to bear the insights of avant-garde art practices and the theoretical elaborations of thinkers like Foucault on the status of social exclusion of women. See also Henry Giroux, *Bordercrossings* (New York: Routledge, 1992).

3. Craig Owen, "The Allegorical Impulse: Toward a Theory of Postmodernism," in *Performance Text(e)s and Documents* (Montreal: Parachute, 1981), p. 47.

4. The full citation from George Mathieu reads as follows: "This new Cosmism which follows humanism will be as responsible as the Occident if it allows itself to be duped by appearances. Never was lucidity won at such cost. You who squeezed the fish of the Hyksos between the calcium deposits, beware of the traps of the new Caesars" (translation from subtitles).

5. Juliet Mitchell and Jacqueline Rose, *Feminine Sexuality: Jacques Lacan and the école freudienne* (New York: Norton, 1983), p. 144.

6. The pun hinges on the German preposition "über," which can be used in conjunction with "lachen" to mean both to laugh about something and to laugh with the whole face. Peter: "Worüber lachst du?" Anna: "Über mein ganzes Gesicht."

7. Mary Ann Doane, *The Desire to Desire: The Woman's Film of the 1940s* (Bloomington: Indiana University Press, 1987), p. 1.

8. Ibid., p. 6.

9. Valie Export, *Dokumentations—Ausstellung des Österreichischen Beitrags zur Biennale Venedig 1980* (Wien: Bundesministerism für Unterricht und Kunst, 1980), p. 13.

10. Tania Modleski, *The Women Who Knew Too Much: Hitchcock and Feminist Theory* (New York: Methuen, 1988), p. 13.

11. Kaja Silverman, *The Acoustic Mirror: The Female Voice in Psychoanalysis and Cinema* (Bloomington: Indiana University Press, 1988), p. 1.

12. Ibid., p. 20.

13. This connection between Freud's essay on "The Uncanny" and *Invisible Adversaries* was central to my article "Through the Eyes of a Woman: Valie Export's Invisible Adversary," published in *Substance* 29, 1983.

14. The story of the Sandman has two main themes, one of which hinges on the traumatization of the child Nathaniel (Hoffmann's spelling: Nathanael) when his father dies in a chemical laboratory accident. The father had been working on an experiment with a mysterious man named Coppelius, who, prior to the accident, had been connected to the tale of the Sandman. Although commonly used to coax children to go to sleep, the story of the Sandman is transformed by Nathaniel's nanny into a gruesome tale that threatens the child with the loss of his eyes. Coppelius's disappearance after the father's death further shrouds his person in mystery in the child's mind.

    The second theme begins with the reappearance of Coppelius as the optometrist Coppola, who happens to sell a pair of binoculars to Nathaniel, now a student and engaged to a loving and intelligent young lady. With the aid of his new binoculars, Nathaniel spies a most wondrous woman across the street from his apartment, with whom he falls in love immediately and who, at a later social occasion, is introduced to him as the daughter of the scientist Spalanzani. Nathaniel's recognition that the woman is in reality a mechanical doll causes him to go mad and fall ill, just as he had when his father died. This pattern is repeated with fatal consequences when he sees Coppola/Coppelius again through his binoculars at a later time.

15. Sigmund Freud, "Das Unheimliche," in *Gesammelte Werke* XII (Frankfurt: Fischer Verlag, 1968), p. 231.

16. E. T. A. Hoffmann, *Werke,* II (Frankfurt: Insel Verlag, 1967), p. 25.

17. It is true that the loving attention Nathaniel lavishes on Olimpia has no bounds. But that aspect is not what astonishes his friends, who take it for granted, as they tell him, that there is no sense in debating the worthiness of the love object. What does surprise them is that Nathaniel seems to have been the only one at the social gathering who did not sense that Olimpia was just a doll. One of his friends questions him to that effect: "Do me a favor, brother . . . tell me how it was possible for such a smart fellow as you are to fall for this waxen face, this wooden doll over there? . . . For the rest of us there is something uncanny about this Olimpia" (32). Nathaniel, however, pities his friends for their lack of imagination and accounts to himself: "Only in Olimpia's love do I find my self again" (p. 33).

18. Sigmund Freud, "Das Unheimliche," p. 242.

19. Nathaniel's move to objectify the live woman ("you damned automaton") only in order to worship the mechanical doll as a goddess might
finally provide the link between psychoanalytic, anthropological, and
Marxist definitions of fetishism.

20. If Freud turns a blind eye to the position of woman in his account of
the uncanny, he is equally blind in his assessment of what he describes
as "the old world-view of animism, which was characterized by the
pre-dominance of the spiritual world, by the narcissistic overestima-
tion of subjective mental processes, the omnipotence of thoughts and
the magical practices based upon this view" ("Das Unheimliche,"
p. 253). The distinction between animism and the castration complex,
Freud initially insists, is of utmost theoretical importance. The
uncanny, which stems from infantile complexes (castration), does not
involve material reality at all since psychic reality has taken its place;
it is a question of the repression of a content and the return of that
repressed content. In opposition to that process, the loss in the reality
of a belief and a restimulation of that belief characterizes the uncanny,
which results from primitive animistic convictions. Although Freud
points out that most experiences of the uncanny occur in the context
of animistic beliefs, he is nevertheless convinced that a person's complete "overcoming" of those beliefs would mean an end to the experience of the uncanny in that order. Yet, in spite of this initial
separation of the uncanny into two types ("primitives" and childhood), Freud turns around to acknowledge the impossibility of distin-
gusihing at all times between the two aspects of the uncanny in lived
experience. Not only is there an intimate relationship between primitive convictions and infantile complexes; Freud goes one step further
when he declares that the former are actually rooted in the latter,
since what is at issue is a form of primary narcissism that pertains to
children as well as to the "primitive phase" of mankind: "It seems
that all of us have gone through a phase in our individual development that corresponds to the animism of the primitives" (p. 253).

The relegation of so-called primitive ways of thinking to infantile
complexes has been challenged in the meantime by anthropological
theory and research. In *The Savage Mind,* for example, Lévi-Strauss
distinguishes magical thought from scientific thought "not so much
by any ignorance or contempt of determinism but by a more imperi-
ous and uncompromising demand for it" (p. 11). Magic, in other
words, is a more totalizing determinism than science. It cannot be
regarded, Lévi-Strauss argues, as the forerunner of science or as science in its incipient stage. On the contrary, magical thought represents
an independent system of acquiring knowledge that differs from science not so much in the kind of mental operation it performs as in the
types of phenomena it selects as important. Because Freud chose to
amalgamate "material," historical reality into the psychic phenomena
of infantile complexes, he missed the chance for the exploration of
real difference.

21. Sigmund Freud, "Das Unheimliche," p. 246.

5. Menschenfrauen

1. Valie Export in conversation.

2. Valie Export, *Austria, Biennale di Venezia* (Vienna: Bundesministerium für Unterricht und Kunst, 1980), p. 95.
3. Kaja Silverman, *The Acoustic Mirror* (Bloomington: Indiana University Press, 1987), p. 188.
4. Domna C. Stanton, "Autobiography: Is the Subject Different?" in *The Female Autograph*, Stanton and Plottel, eds. (New York: New York Library Forum, 1984), p. 6.
5. Ibid.
6. Sidonie Smith, *A Poetics of Women's Autobiography* (Bloomington: Indiana UP, 1987), p. 52.
7. Ibid., p. 56.
8. Ibid., p. 58.
9. Ibid., p. 59.
10. Helke Sander, "Die Madonna mit der Kreissage," in *Frauen in der Kunst* I, Nabakowski, Sander, Gorsen, eds. (Frankfurt: Suhrkamp, 1980), p. 64.
11. Valie Export, Export Archive.
12. *Variety* (October 30, 1980).

6. *The Practice of Love*

1. Hannah Arendt, *On Violence* (New York: Harcourt Brace, 1969, 1970), p. 80.
2. Roland Barthes, *A Lover's Discourse,* trans. Richard Howard. (New York: Hill and Wang, 1978), p. 44.
3. Julia Kristeva, *Tales of Love,* trans. by Leon S. Roudiez (New York: Columbia UP, 1987), p. 65.
4. Jean Baudrillard, *The Evil Demon of Images* (Sydney: The Power Institute of Fine Arts, 1988), p. 45.
5. Sigmund Freud, *Das Unbehagen in der Kultur* (Frankfurt: Fischer, 1970), p. 129, translation my own.
6. Ibid., p. 107.
7. The translation of this and other brief passages from the film text is taken from the subtitles with only minor changes.
8. Jessica Benjamin, *The Bonds of Love* (New York: Pantheon, 1988), p. 31.
9. Ibid., p. 46–47.
10. Ibid.
11. Donna J. Haraway, *Simians, Cyborgs, and Women* (New York: Routledge, 1991), p. 180.

7. *Syntagma*

1. Kaja Silverman, *The Acoustic Mirror* (Bloomington: Indiana UP, 1988), p. 50.
2. Sigrid Weigel, " Double Focus," in *Feminist Aesthetics*, ed. Gisela Ecker (Boston: Beacon, 1985), pp. 59–80.
3. Mary Ann Doane, *The Desire to Desire: The Woman's Film of the 1940s* (Bloomington: Indiana UP, 1987), p. 23.
4. Sigrid Weigel, "Traum—Stadt—Frau," *Die Unwirklichkeit der Stadte,* ed. Klaus Scherpe (Reinbek: Rowohlt, 1988), p. 173.
5. Susan Merrill Squier, Introduction to *Women Writers and the City* (Knoxville: University of Tennessee Press, 1984), p. 5.

6. Mark Seltzer, *Bodies and Machines* (New York: Routledge, 1992), p. 17.

7. Jean Baudrillard, "The Year 2000 Has Already Happened," in *Body Invaders: Panic Sex in America,* ed. Arthur and Marilouise Kroker (New York: St. Martin's, 1987), p. 43.

8. Charles Levin, "Carnal Knowledge of Aesthetic States," in *Body Invaders,* p. 100.

9. Teresa de Lauretis, *Technologies of Gender* (Bloomington: Indiana UP, 1987), p. 32.

10. Diana Fuss, *Essentially Speaking* (New York: Routledge, 1989), p. 21.

11. Valie Export, "The Real and Its Double: The Body," in *Discourse* 11, 1 (Fall–Winter 1988–89), pp. 3–27.

1989

Die Meta-Morphose (The Meta-Morphosis). Screenplay written in collaboration with Roswitha Mueller.

Aktionkunst International (Actionism International); video (73 min.). Written in 1988, directed by Valie Export. ORF Vienna "Kunst-Stücke," broadcast on WDR in August 1989. Interviews with Vito Acconci, Jean Baudrillard, Karen Finley, Dick Higgins, Allan Kaprow, Otto Muehl, Gina Pane, Mark Pauline (Survival Research Laboratories), Gerhard Rühm, Carolee Schneeman, Wolf Vostell. (Review by Joachim Hauschild, "Fernsehen bildet." *Süddeutsche Zeitung* 4/3/89.)

1987

Maschinenkörper–Körperraum–Körpermaschinen (Machine-Bodies/ Body-Space/Body-Machines). Computer film (12 min.). In Process.

Unica (Dunkler Frühling) [Unica (Dark Spring)]. Feature film, in process. Segments of the life of Unica Zurn as woman, artist, model, and medium, played by different women of different ages.

Mental Images, Oder der Zugang der Welt (Mental Images, or, the Gateway to the World). Computer film, collaborative work. Produced by mental images, Berlin. Awards: 1987—Prix Ars electronica (2d place); Nico Graphic, Tokyo (3rd); Broadcast Frankfurt/G (2d). 1988—NCGA (noncommercial, 1st place).

Alaska, Anagrammatischer Film (Alaska, Anagrammatic Film). In process. The identities, lives, work, ideas, etc., of five women, collapsed anagrammatically into one another.

1986

Yukon Quest; video documentary (45 min.). Collaboration with Ingrid Wiener, Oswald Wiener, Elly Forster. ORF/Vienna "Kunst-Stücke." Berlin International Film Festival, Panorama, 1987.

Ein perfektes Paar oder die Unzucht wechselt ihre Haut (A Perfect Pair, or, Indecency Sheds Its Skin). Video (12 min.). Screenplay, production, and direction by Valie Export. Produced within the framework of the ZDF production "Seven Women—Seven Sins." "Das kleine Fernsehspiel" (a program slot on German television featuring low-budget independent films). Broadcast in 1987. The seven contributors to the video are Chantal Akerman, Maxi Cohen, Valie Export, Laurence Gavron, Bette Gordon, Helke Sander, Ulrike Ottinger. Award: Annual Daniel Wadsworth Memorial Video Festival, Festival Prize 1988. U. S. Video Rental: Video Data, New York City (Home Video Market). U. S. Film Rental: 16 mm film, Maxi Cohen, New York City.

Die Zweiheit der Natur (The Duality of Nature). Video (2 min.). Collaboration with F. Praschek, produced by Valie Export. Ars Electronica/ORF.

1985

Tischbemerkungen–November 1985 (Table Quotes–November 1985). 16 mm film (45 min.). Documentary about Oswald Wiener. ORF/Vienna "Kunst-Stücke." Premiered at the Berlin International Film Festival, Panorama, 1986.

1984

Die Praxis der Liebe (The Practice of Love). 35 mm feature film (90 min.). Screenplay (written 1982) and direction by Valie Export. Entered at the Berlin International Film Festival, 1985. Honorable Mention: Tyneside International Film Festival, 1985. Discussed by Brenda Longfellow in "Sex/Textual Politics: Tracing the Imaginary in the Works of Valie Export," in *Borderline* (Montreal, 1986). Produced by Valie Export (A)/Kongismark & Wullenweber (FRG). U. S. Video Rental: Facets Video, Chicago.

1983

Syntagma; 16 mm experimental film (18 min.). Screenplay and direction by Valie Export. Produced by Valie Export. Honorable mention at the 31st Oberhausen West German Film Festival of 1985. (See Katharina Sykora in "31. Westdeutsche Filmtage Oberhausen," 1985.) Special Jury's Prize, 27th Bilbao International Film Festival, 1985. U. S. Rental: Foreign Images, Evanston/ Chicago, IL.

1982

Das bewaffnete Auge (The Armed Eye). Video documentary. Documentary about international avant-garde and experimental film. Script and presentation by Valie Export. ORF/Vienna, "Kunst-Stücke." Broadcast in 1983.

1979

Menschenfrauen. 16 mm feature film (100 min.). Directed and produced by Valie Export, written by Peter Weibel and Valie Export. Premiered at the Berlin International Film Festival, International Forum for Young Filmmakers, 1980. (See Gary Indiana's discussion *East Village Eye*, New York, January 1982). U. S. Video Rental: Facts Video, Chicago.

Restringierter Code (Restricted Code). Videotape of performance, *Restringierter Code*, a body-inter-action at the Städtische Galerie of the Lenbachhaus, Munich. Produced by P. A. P. Munich.

1978

I [(Beat) It]. Videotape of performance, *I [(Beat) It]*, a body performance at the Mike Steiner Gallery, Berlin. Produced by Michael Steiner.

1977

Delta. Ein Stück (Delta: A Piece). Videotape of performance, *Delta: A Piece*, a body/persona performance at the Cologne Kunstmarkt. Produced by P. A. P., Munich.

1976

Unsichtbare Gegner (Invisible Adversaries). 16 mm feature film (112 min.). Produced and directed by Valie Export. Screenplay by Peter Weibel with Valie Export, based on an outline by Valie Export. Premiered at the Berlin International Film Festival, the International Forum for Young Filmmakers, 1977. Prizewinner at the 1978 Mostra Internazionale de Film d'Autore, San Remo; awarded a special prize by the jury. Honorable Mention as Outstanding Film of the Year, London International Film Festival, 1978. See Jim Hoberman, "Ten Best: Balance of Trade," *Village Voice*, 1982. U. S. Video Rental: Facets Video, Chicago.

Homometer II. Videotape of performance of *Homometer II*, body action, street action, transsocial communication, Vienna.

Wann ist der Mensch eine Frau? (When Is a Human Being a Woman?). Persona video (15 min.).

Schnitte (Cuts). Video (10 min.), Vienna.

1974

Raumsehen und Raumhören (Seeing Space and Hearing Space). Video of action, *Raumsehen und Raumhören*, within the context of the exhibit "Art Remains Art: Aspects of International Art in the Early 1970s," Project 1974, Cologne Kunstverein. Time statue, space statue, melody, 20 min. Sound by Christian Michelis and Valie Export.

Body Politics. Video (2 min.), performance, Vienna.

1973

. . . Remote . . . Remote . . . . 16 mm avant-garde film, film action (12 min.).

Mann & Frau & Animal (Man and Woman and Animal). 16 mm avant-garde film (12 min.).

Adjungierte Dislokationen (Adjoined Dislocations). Experimental film, spatial film; one 16 mm film and two 8 mm films with triple projection (10 min.).

Asemie (Asemia). Videotape of performance *Asemie, or the Inability to Express Oneself through MIENENSPIEL*, body action, body–material interaction, Vienna.

Hyperbulie (Hyperbulia). Videotape of performance *Hyperbulia*, body action, body–material interaction, Vienna.

Sehtext: Fingergedicht (Sight Poem: Finger Poem). Video following the 1968 photo series Finger Poem. Video-poem (2 min.), Vienna.

Die süsse Nummer: Ein Konsumerlebnis (The Sweet One: A Consumer Experience). Video following the consumer poem of 1968, (10 min.). Consumer literature. Vienna.

Hauchtext: Liebesgedicht (1970) (Love Poem). Video poem, screen action (3 min.). Vienna.

Touching (1970). Video. Space video, screen action (2 min.). Vienna.

1971–72

Interrupted Line. Avant-garde film, time and space film, simulation (9 min.). Vienna.

Stille Sprache (Silent Language). Persona performance. Performance of historical representations of women. Vienna.

1971

Facing a Family. Television action, video. Imaginary television screen. Total art: social structure versus the structure of art, variations of structure, transsocial communication, sociological model. Meta-cinema, film without film. (5–20 min.) Broadcast of ORF/Vienna, "Kontakt."

Eros/ion. Intermedia metafilm. Concrete materials, abstract signs. Film beyond film, film without film. Materials: plate glass, powdered glass, glass splinters, snow or paper, naked human bodies.

1970

Split Reality. Video poem after a demonstration, 1967. Intermedia. Expanded cinema, reduction through doubling (3 min.). Sound and image, record player, monitor.

1969

Tonfilm (Sound Film). Environment simulation, electronic cinema. Materials: photoelectric amplifier, glottis, light-sensitive resistance, amplifiers, light and nonlight. Sound film—a film to be heard.

Das magische Auge (The Magical Eye). Collaboration with Peter Weibel. Intermedia expanded movie. Autogenerative sound screen. Materials: PVC screen, light-sensitive resistances, films, people. Underground explosion within the context of "War, Art, Riot," Munich, Cologne, Frankfurt. Sponsor: K. H. Hein, Munich.

Eine Reise ist eine Reise wert (A Journey Is Worth the Trip). Collaboration with Peter Weibel. Structural film, 8 mm travel film (8 min.).

Proselyt (Proselyte). Environment simulation, Expanded movie. Materials: retinal rays, human eyes, consciousness, cinema screening room, "reality."

1968

Auf+Ab+An+Zu (Up+Down+On+Off). Film action, active screen, film as determined reflex. 8 mm, 3 min. Materials: drawing implements, film and painting, actor, stabile film/drawing screen. This film is a teaching film, an exercise in painting, an echo of the cubist desertion of painting. Space is conceptualized as an instance in time. The liberated observer, who must take part in the reproduction of the film, adds to what has been painted onto the celluloid with his/her drawing pencil. The simultaneity of projection and montage that is accomplished on the screen rather than on the celluloid shows that montage is drawing.

Vorspann. Ein Lesefilm (Cast and Credits: A Film to Be Read). 16 mm, 12 min. The film consists of cast and credits, titles, descriptions of material, dates of origin, introductions, credits, etc., that precede different film stories. This film is dedicated to Export's daughter Perdita as a reading exercise.

Ping Pong. Local film, television film, screen action, film object, film action/action film. 8 mm, 3 min. Materials: Ping-Pong paddles, Ping-Pong balls, actress, stabile film screen, television screen. Prize winner at the 3rd Maraisiade, Vienna, for most political film.

333. Simulation projection, cinema project, expanded movie. Triple projection specified. Materials: three 8 mm film projectors, three rotating screen sections (tinted, of different materials), patter films.

Tapp und Tast Kino (Touch Cinema). The first mobile women's film, expanded cinema. Feminist actionism, transsocial communication, real cinema, street film, sociological model/action, body action. Skin film, 33 sec. Material: Human mini-screen, mini-cinema, actress, visitor, premiered at the Maraisiade, Vienna.

Splitscreen–Solipsismus. Film installation. Expanded movie, reduction through doubling, two images with one projector. 8 mm, 3 min. Material: Aluminum foil, screen.

Ansprache Aussprache (Speak to, Speak Out). Home movie. Expanded movie, transsocial communication, active screen, 3 min., 8 mm. Material: transparent screen, microphone, loneliness.

Gesichtsgrimassen (Facial Grimaces). 8 mm, 1 min.

Wor(l)d Cinema: Ein Sprachfest [Wor(l)d Cinema: A Festival of Languages]. Collaboration with Peter Weibel, partially finished 1973.

Valie Export. Collaboration with Peter Weibel, object film, film object. Materials: transparent PVC foil with a portrait of Valie Export.

Instant Film. Collaboration with Peter Weibel. Object film, expanded movie. Material: transparent PVC foil.

Ein Familienfilm von Waltraud Lehner (A Family Film by Waltraud Lehner). Expanded movie, interaction between people and cinema. 8 mm, 30 min. Material: portable microphone.

Ohne Titel xn (Without Title xn). Collaboration with Peter Weibel. Environment film.

Der Kuss (The Kiss). Collaboration with Peter Weibel. Expanded movie, slow-motion picture. Material: two actresses, flashlights.

Ohne Titel Nr. 2 (Without Title No. 2). Collaboration with Peter Weibel, environment film. Material: multidimensional objects, pattern films.

1967–68

Cutting. Expanded cinema, intermedia, film action, multimedia. Screens: skin screens, paper screen, material screen.

Abstract Film No. 1. Expanded movie, film action. Land art. Environment simulation, environment cinema. Basic elements: Water, fire, earth, air. Materials: mirror, water, thick and thin fluid, colored material, flashlights, cinema screen, nature screen.

Ars Lucis. Movie environment. Mirror/prism environment, multimedia. Materials: film projectors, films, slide projectors, turntables, cylindrical prisms, stationary and movable mirrors, different projection surfaces in various positions and curvatures.

1967

Menstruationsfilm (Menstruation Film). 8 mm, 3 min., Lugano, Switzerland.

INDEX

Page numbers in italics refer to photographs.

241

ROSWITHA MUELLER, Associate Professor of German and Comparative Literature at the University of Wisconsin, Milwaukee, is the author of *Bertolt Brecht and the Theory of Media* and coeditor of the journal *Discourse*.